Rhonnie & Andrew,
her inseparable Senegalese parrot.

WEST
AFRICA
CALLING

"Go therefore and make disciples of all nations, baptizing them in the name of the Father and of the Son and of the Holy Spirit, teaching them to observe all that I have commanded you. And behold, I am with you always, to the end of the age."

                                        Matthew 19:14 ESV

WEST AFRICA CALLING

By Stanley David King
May 1927-March 2020

West Africa Calling

Copyright©2021 Ahelia Publishing

All Rights Reserved. No part of this book may be reproduced in any form without written permission of the publisher.

Unless otherwise indicated, all Scriptures are taken from …

Scriptures marked NIV are taken from the NEW INTERNATIONAL VERSION (NIV): Scripture taken from THE HOLY BIBLE, NEW INTERNATIONAL VERSION ®. Copyright© 1973, 1978, 1984, 2011 by Biblica, Inc.TM. Used by permission of Zondervan

ISBN# 978-1-988001-55-5

1. God 2. Christianity 3. Religion 4. Missions 5. West Africa

Printed in the United States of America
Published in the United States of America

www.aheliapublishing.com

Stan, Rhonnie, Phyllis, 1954

Lovingly dedicated to the memory of the late Phyllis King, beloved wife, and Rhonwen Wenden-King, daughter.

TABLE OF CONTENTS

1	My Early Years	pg. 16
2	The Family Tree	pg. 23
3	Childhood Memories	pg. 26
4	A New Dad	pg. 33
5	My Life Was Changed	pg. 38
6	Trying To Forget God	pg. 47
7	Further Preparations	pg. 51
8	Back To Bible School	pg. 57
9	Goodbye Canada	pg. 60
10	Gai Paree	pg. 64
11	Alliance Francaise	pg. 67
12	Life At Madame Vexiau's	pg. 71
13	Adjusting	pg. 75
14	My Wife To Be	pg. 81
15	Wedding Bells	pg. 87
16	Ministry With Youth For Christ	pg. 93
17	Ministry In Portugal	pg. 100
18	Ministry In Paris And Ireland	pg. 107
19	Big Surprise Comes In Small Package	pg. 115
20	Return To Canada	pg. 122
21	Africa Still Calls	pg. 135
22	The Enemy Strikes Again	pg. 139
23	The Day Has Arrived	pg. 148
24	History of Upper Volta/Burkina Faso	pg. 151
25	Arrival In Upper Volta	pg. 156
26	Storms Off The Sahara	pg. 159
27	Filling In At Kassou	pg. 162
28	We Choose The Sissala People	pg. 168
29	Searching For Answers	pg. 175

30	A New Beginning	pg. 179
31	God Confirms The Preaching Of His Word	pg. 182
32	Bible Training Center	pg. 185
33	Extended Furlough	pg. 192
34	Young Men Whose Hearts God Touched	pg. 197
35	Bible Translation	pg. 201
36	Old Things Have Passed Away	pg. 204
37	The Power Of The Enemy	pg. 208
38	God Answers Prayer	pg. 212
39	A Safe Home For Teen-Aged Girls	pg. 216
40	Visit To Ghana	pg. 220
41	The Circle Is Complete	pg. 230

| Editor's Note | pg. 239 |

| Appendix: Rhonnie's Story | pg. 248 |

*** Ahelia Publishing has not fully edited this manuscript. We, and those who brought this manuscript to us, have agreed it is in the best interest and desire of Stan himself, to leave it (as much as possible) in his own words.

Forward

Papa King, (Stan), as he is known to most of us in Burkina Faso is many things to many people. Apostle to the Sissala people, evangelist, pastor, counselor, mediator, messenger of peace, healer, miracle worker, prophet, medical doctor, professor, universal father, prince, taxi driver, Nasara, tubabu, etc. Papa King was all these things to all these people and even more.

On account of the life-giving presence of Mama and Papa King in Sub-Saharan Africa, we are bold to say, "The people living in darkness have seen a great light; and for those living in the land of the shadow of death, a light has dawned."

A long-distance runner in the struggle for a better quality of life for all, Stan's journey is rooted in a rich Apostolic and missional tradition that puts a premium on Pioneering work, personal sacrifice, gentle embrace of others, cultural manners and social justice. Though perennially scarred by the traumatic life turns that paved the realities of his own upbringing, Papa King emerged with great dignity, decency and integrity; with love, courage and humour; choosing social advocacy rather than a life of blind avarice and personal subservience. Ironically, the sum realities of chronic trauma and vicious stigma of his earlier "soul-making" yielded his true passion to profoundly show his fellow human what is good—to do justly and to love mercy, and to walk humbly with his God.

As one deeply and profoundly transformed by Papa and Mama King's apostolic ministry, I can honestly testify with the millions of people whose lives have been uplifted: that, "In their light, we saw light." Papa King (Stan) was known for his advocacy for the little guy everywhere, male or female, or hermaphrodite, no matter the colour of their skin or eyes, how humble a beginning, wealth or poverty. Under the gigantic tree that Papa and Mama King's lives represented, Pastors and flock alike found manna and refuge under its shadows, from the long walk in the plight of the world which God so loved that He gave His only Son, whosoever believes in Him might not perish but have everlasting life.

I wept as I read the story Stan told in Chapter 31 (GOD CONFIRMS THE PREACHING OF HIS WORD). It is a story that took place one Friday night in a little village called Yoro, my paternal village: The men were sitting out in front of the huts looking glum. Pierre (my Father) said they were waiting for us, so we could pray for one of the women who had been in labour for three days and still hadn't given birth. They led Abraham and me into a dark room, lit only by the flame from a clay saucer filled with oil. As my eyes became accustomed to the dark, I made out the form of three women. One lady was lying naked on the floor with the other ladies each holding one of her arms. A large log lay in front of her. I looked for signs of her breathing but could see none. Was she already dead? These two women had been dragging the young mother on her stomach over the log, trying to force the baby to be born.

Both Abraham and I prayed for the woman, then we went out to start the service. Shortly after, there was a lot of commotion, with women coming and going. Pierre informed us that everything was fine now—the baby had been born, although dead, and the mother was up and doing fine. The people who had come for the service from Yoro and near-by villages were all talking excitedly. Later, Pierre told me they were all moved by such a demonstration of power. The news soon circulated, and we had Chiefs coming from several villages to our door, asking if we could come to their village to tell them about the God of such power. "Where can we find such power as this?" they exclaimed, "Our idols do not have it!"

There is something prophetic in this story. To me, the woman represents the Church of Africa in labour—the church he gave the shirt off his back to serve. The baby had been born, although dead, and the mother was up and doing fine. That stillborn is not her last. That woman conceived again and again by the Power of the Holy Spirit. The Church may have suffered many dangers, toils and storms, but thanks be to God, she is not barren. That woman gave birth to me, and the many, and we are deeply grateful for those who sowed the seed of the gospel at the expense of their lives.

I bow my head to pay tribute to one of ACOP's finest missionaries. To our fellowship, the Apostolic Church of Pentecost, behold the testament of a grateful people from the field where your sons were, by all means, martyrs of the faith; I owe my life.

Stan most wanted the world to encounter the Lord through the story of his life. He wanted his humble story to be an inspiration for a new generation of missionaries.

We now come full circle. He was the missionary in Africa. Because of him, I met the Lord. Now, I am a missionary right back in the same country that sent him out. I journeyed with Stan during the last chapter of his earthly life. He never missed encouraging me and asking about the work in Africa. We never parted till he bragged about the photos in his room... the love that shaped his passion and deference, the memory of the late Phyllis King, beloved wife, and Rhonwen Wenden-King, daughter. He was ecstatic about his granddaughter and "great-grandchildren". His filial love for Travis and Tammy cannot go overlooked. He reminded me of his love for and spoke of them as his own children. The entrustment of this seminal work to Travis & Tammy is one of his last wishes fulfilled.

Before I close, let me echo and paraphrase the words of a father, the word of E.G. Bradley, then chairman of the Missionary Council of the Apostolic Church of Pentecost in 1983, as he dedicated an earlier book called *Setting Captives Free* by Armien H. Hildebrand whom Papa King spoke about in this book. On Pentecost morning in the streets of Jerusalem, a humanity redeeming chain reaction was started. The divine energy generated caused further reactions that are still bringing life-changing benefits to a needy world today.

Truly one of the most significant stages for God's mighty acts was manifest in Upper Volta, now Burkina Faso. Here, divinely chosen and empowered human instruments from various walks of life have sown seeds from which sprung a great multitude of believers. Burkina Faso is not just another national church in a distant land, but one that has become a missionary hub with spokes leading in all directions. This book tells how it all began through the lenses of Papa King.

This book will get to your heart. None of the facts are exaggerated or embellished for the work of this man needed no embellishment. As you read this book you will find your faith growing, your desire for the power of God increasing and your concern for lost souls deepening. When this starts to happen, hand over your life afresh to God and be prepared to do whatever He tells you to do. The Holy Spirit will use you, as He has used Papa and Mama King, to touch the lives of others and help to reach a lost world for Jesus Christ.

A great beginning has no end.

Toward unfeigned love, still becoming, always, The Most Reverend Daniel Zopoula. Archbishop, CEEC, The Miz City Church, Lethbridge, Alberta

Chapter 1

MY EARLY YEARS

I CAME INTO THIS WORLD ON MAY 25TH, 1927, IN Eston—a small prairie town situated in one of the best wheat-growing areas in Saskatchewan—about 215 kilometers southwest of Saskatoon. My Dad was a grain buyer for the Saskatchewan Pool in the small hamlet of Plato, about 24 Kilometers east of Eston. About midmorning on that day, Mom sent word to Dad that she was having labour pains and they would have to get to Eston as quickly as possible. It was pouring rain and none of the roads were graded—let alone paved—in those days. It was tough slugging through the water and mud, and then within 6 kilometers of Eston, Dad got stuck in a slough. What happened next, I'm not sure. The farmer on the west side of the slough pulled dad out of the mud with a team of horses. However, I am uncertain as to whether Mother was still in the car, or whether Dr. McInnis, the Doctor at Eston, had driven out, picked her up, and taken her to the Hospital.

In any case, Mom arrived in time and I was born in the old wooden Eston Union Hospital. My older sister, Bess, had been born on March 24, 1924, in Grandma Shuttleworth's home in the Hamlet of Isham. Dad and Mom were farming in the area at that time. My second sister, Thelma, was born on December 10, 1925, in Grandma King's home in Plato, where Dad was now working as the Saskatchewan Pool Agent.

(Sidebar/footnote: In 1916 the Saskatchewan Government passed the Union Hospital Act, realizing the need for rural hospitals to keep pace with the growing rural population. In 1917, the R.M. of Snipe Lake and the town of Eston opened a 10-bed hospital in Eston, becoming the first one to be built and operated in the province. In 1930, a wing was added to the hospital doubling its capacity. In 1952 the hospital burned to the ground. The Eston Legion Memorial Hall became an emergency hospital and served the community for the next two and a half years. In 1955, a brick 24-bed hospital was opened, but in 1993, the Romanow NDP government shut down 52 hospitals, the Eston Union Hospital being one of them. The sturdy, imposing hospital building still stands empty on Main Street to this day.)

Shortly after my birth, we moved back to the Isham area where Dad and Mom teamed up with Mom's two brothers, Alvin and David, on the Shuttleworth farm. Two years later, my Dad passed away in the Sanatorium in Saskatoon after a short bout with a tubercular kidney. One kidney had been removed and the other one failed. He was just 29 years old and Mom was left with three young kids to care for. She relocated to a house that Granddad Shuttleworth had moved onto a lot next to the store and Post Office that he ran in Isham.

The year I turned 6, we moved into the town of Eston and rented a house on 5th Avenue, the south edge of Eston at that time. I took all my schooling in the old, two-story, six-classroom, brick school, graduating in 1945. I liked school but loved sports more than I liked studying. I remember while in grade 5, my sister, Thelma, offered me fifty cents if I improved my grades. That was a lot of money in those days, so I did and kept making good marks right through to Grade 12, graduating with honours.

A Boy Scout Troop started when I was about 12. It was disbanded after only a couple of years, when the Scout Master, the Lutheran Minister, moved from Eston. A year later Air Cadets came to town, with local men taking much of the instructing in such things as fighter plane recognition, metrology, Morse code and Semaphore signaling. Periodically Air Force personnel came by to teach new marching formations and check us on all the things we had been taught. One year we spent two weeks on the Vulcan, Alberta, Air Force Base. While there I had my first ride in an aircraft, the old stalwart trainer, Avro Anson. I went early each morning to the hangar where the pilots were practicing takeoff and landing and had several rides. One British pilot even let me take the controls for a few minutes. In 1944 the Air Cadets were disbanded, as Canada was no longer recruiting for the armed services.

When we first moved to Eston we attended the United Church as a family. Two years later, we moved to a house located where the Post Office now stands. Our next-door neighbors were Rev. and Mrs. Joseph Phillips and their two children, Joseph and Pauline. Rev. Phillips was Pastor of the Eston Assemblies of God church. Although Joseph Jr., was a couple of years older, we became good friends. For some time, I begged Mom to let me go to the Assembly of God Church, and finally, she relented. I was 8 years old when I started attending. Not long afterward, my two sisters and then Mom started to attend. Meetings were being held in a clapboard building that had been built on the north-east corner of Main Street and 2nd Avenue, where the Town Office is now located. As the church was affiliated with the American Assemblies of God, many preachers came for evangelistic or Bible teaching meetings. On many a Sunday, missionaries would share their call and their ministry to various countries of the world.

These missionary meetings had a profound effect on me as a teenager, and I often thought that one day I would like to be a missionary in some foreign country. I went to the altar on several occasions as a teenager, and even though I prayed the sinner's prayer with all sincerity, I never received any assurance of salvation. Many times, I was under strong conviction and I remember a couple of events that made me wonder if the rapture had taken place, and the fear I felt when I thought Christ had come and I had been left behind. When I was thirteen, the Phillips family moved away. My other friends were not Christians, and although I continued to attend church, I no longer made time for spiritual things. I tried to forget the Lord, but I found out later that the Lord had never forgotten me.

Bess, Stan, Thelma

Chapter 2
THE FAMILY TREE

GRANDPA AND GRANDMA KING ARRIVED IN CANADA from England in 1911 with four children: my Dad, Roy, who was 8 years old, my Aunt Reca, 6, my Uncle Sidney, 4, and my Aunt Emma, who was 1 year old. The family settled in Moose Jaw where Grandpa's brother, Ted, lived. My Aunt Hazel was born there in 1913. Grandpa moved the family to a farm in the Plato area. My Dad, being the oldest of the kids, was needed to help on the farm. Consequently, he was not able to attend school on a regular basis. He taught himself to play the saxophone and violin and was much in demand to play at local dances. When his parents moved into the town of Plato, Dad rented land and a two-room shack in the area that later became the Hamlet of Isham.

Granddad Shuttleworth was born in Ontario and came west to work on a farm at Cavalier, North Dakota, where he met and married Grandma. My Aunty Olive and Mom were born in Bathgate, a nearby town with a hospital. That makes me a first-generation Canadian. Granddad decided to try farming in Arcola—in southern Saskatchewan—and had machinery shipped from Ontario. He remained for three years, but drought finally drove him out. During this time, my two uncles, Alvin and David, were born. Granddad then applied for, and was granted, a homestead in what later became the Isham area. The first Post Office in the area was in the house Granddad built on the homestead. A school was needed, but Government regulations stated there had to be a minimum of 8 students, six years and older, to form a School District. Five-year-old Uncle Dave conveniently became a six-year-old and Ormley School was built in 1912. In 1925 a spur rail line was built from Eston to White Bear and a small hamlet grew when three grain elevators were built along the track. The Ormely School was moved into town. Later, when it was replaced with a new building, Granddad Shuttleworth had the old building moved to Main Street and it became a general store and Post Office. Granddad proposed "Isham" as the name of the new Hamlet. It was built on farmland that was being rented by my Dad.

The King farm and Shuttleworth farm were very close together. Mom spent so much time at the King farm that she was considered one of the family. In her late teens, Mom took nurses training at the Sanatorium in Fort Qu'Appelle and the hospital in Scot, sponsored by the University of Saskatchewan. The plan was to prepare a group of young women to go to Red Cross outposts in the northern parts of the province. Dad was living alone, batching and trying to farm when Mom came home on a weekend after completing the course. He proposed and Mom accepted, thus ending her nursing career. My older sister, Bess, was born in Grandma Shuttleworth's home on the homestead. Soon an opportunity to operate a Pool Elevator came up, and the family moved to Plato. Grandpa and Grandma King had moved off the farm into Plato, and my second sister, Thelma, was born in Grandma King's home. A year and a half later, I joined the family. After Dad passed away, Grandpa and Grandma King moved back to Moose Jaw, where my Aunt Dorothy was born. They next moved to a wooded acreage near the town of Wonnock, BC, and later, Grandpa became the manager of an apartment block in Mission, BC. They then moved back to Saskatchewan to live with their oldest daughter, Reca, in Kindersley. Grandma soon was moved to the Seniors' Home in Elrose, where she passed away. Grandpa continued to live with Reca until he, too, passed away. They are buried in the Kindersley Cemetery.

Granddad and Grandma Shuttleworth ran the General Store and Post Office until they were advised to move to the BC coast for medical reasons. Grandma almost died from a severe case of asthma, but the moist BC air gave her relief and she lived into her 90s. Granddad passed away several years earlier. They are both buried in a cemetery in Vancouver.

Chapter 3
Childhood Memories

I DON'T REMEMBER MUCH OF LIFE IN PLATO OR EVEN later when we moved back on the farm near Isham. The house where my Uncles lived was a two-story structure--one large room serving as a kitchen and eating area on the main floor and one bedroom on the upper floor. Dad attached a lean-to to the older building that added two bedrooms and a living room. A trap door in the kitchen floor led to a cellar used as a cool room for storage. Dad loved to make ginger beer, and one night got a bottle from the cellar as a bedtime treat. Somehow, the coal oil lamp got knocked over and the spilled coal oil caught fire. Bess was backing away from the flames toward the open cellar door when Dad made a dash and caught her just before she fell into the hole.

The fall of the year I turned three, Dad was hauling coal to fill up the coal shed before winter. Mom checked to see that all three of us kids were in the house when she saw Dad drive into the yard with a truckload of coal. She said that it seemed only seconds later that she turned around and I was gone. She ran to the door and screamed for Dad to stop. I had run outside and hidden behind the coal shed door. Dad had backed so that the truck box was pushing up against the door. I was jammed so tightly by the door that I could not move. Dad didn't dare release the brake for fear the truck might roll backward and crush my skull. With his foot against the wall and pulling on the door with all his strength, Dad could barely spring it enough for Mom to pull me out, scraping the skin on both temples as she did so. Just as He promised, Heavenly Father sent guardian angels just in time for my sister and me!

Both my Aunt Emma, (aka Sliv), and my Aunt Hazel, (aka Hay), were schoolteachers. On several occasions, before school ended in June, Aunt Sliv would pick me up and I would stay with her in the teacherage until school was out. A young man from Wartime, Roy Wiggins, was courting her and I got the idea that when he came, it was to play with me. Apparently, I put on quite a show, playing with Roy, until, exasperated, he would make me lie down and would lie down beside me until I fell asleep so that they could have some uninterrupted time together. When the school year ended, Aunt Sliv would be joined by Aunt Hay, and together, they would drive in their Essex car to Moose Jaw where I would stay the summer with Grandpa and Grandma King. There were ball diamonds across the street, and I used to be a one-man baseball team. I would hit an imaginary ball with an imaginary bat, run around first and slide into second. Then I would be an outfielder, catch the ball and throw to the catcher. I would run to home plate and slide in safely. Aunt Hay said I would play like that for hours. One evening as I was watching a real softball game, I heard a lot of cheering going on up the street. The softball players stopped the game and headed up the street, and, curious, I followed along.

We walked a few blocks to a baseball diamond where a crowd had already filled the bleachers. It turned out to be a donkey baseball game. Every player was riding a donkey. The batter swung a large paddle and if he hit the ball, he had to ride the donkey to first. The opposing team had to catch the ball or chase it on a donkey and try to throw the batter out. It was hilarious watching the players trying to get the donkeys to cooperate, and needless to say, it took a long time to play the game which only lasted 3 or 4 innings. My Aunties were frantic when they no longer saw me across the street and started a search. Hearing the roar of the crowd in the distance, they went to investigate. They spotted me sitting on the railing at the very top of the grandstand. I was six years old.

My Aunt Dorothy (aka Pip), liked to sunbathe in the back yard with her girlfriends, and when they had had enough sun, they would lie on the floor of an 8' X 8' tent. I had noticed that there were a dozen or more daddy longlegs spiders in two of the corners of the tent. After the girls were lying down, I beat on the tent corners with a broom, sending the spiders flying. The shrieks from the girls were ear-splitting as they came bounding out of the tent, swatting at the spiders. Fortunately, my Grandpa had seen the whole thing and came to my rescue or my life might have ended right there.

Before Mom decided to move to Eston from Isham, I somehow acquired a pair of skates. There was a frozen water puddle across the road from Granddad's store where I learned to skate. When we moved to Eston, all my free time was spent at the rink. Every Saturday morning there was hockey and, most afternoons and evenings, public skating. As there was no artificial ice in those days, it took very cold weather to make ice in the rink, and often there was no skating until into December. The slough where Dad got stuck the day I was born had ice before the rink. After supper, several of us kids would walk the five kilometers to the slough, carrying our skates, and join the older ones fortunate enough to have access to a vehicle. We were always able to get a ride home after an evening of skating. Eston boasted a rather good senior hockey team that provided good hockey until 1940 when Canada started recruiting young men for the armed forces. The junior hockey team moved up to fill the gap and played surrounding teams almost every week during the winter months. I started as the goalie, but, preferring the action, moved up to center a line on which our town Doctor, Dr. Stewart Holmes, played left wing. Someone on the team suggested we call ourselves the "Ramblers". That name stuck and to this day the Eston Ramblers are a force to be reckoned with around the province.

I loved to sing, and often, when no one was home I would sing at the top of my lungs. I learned hymns and as I would sing them, would imagine myself singing at a Billy Graham Crusade. The town used to have a variety night in the town hall, as there was a lot of talent in the area. Two young gals and a friend and I formed a quartet and sang at these nights. I guess we were fairly good, as we often got invited to sing at other functions as well. A music teacher moved to town to teach violin. I had my Dad's violin that hadn't been used since he passed away. I think it was because my sister, Bess, played the piano for the teacher that she undertook to teach me violin for free. She began a stringed orchestra and put on a yearly concert. Although I was not very good, she allowed me to play in the orchestra. Soon after she left Eston, both my sisters, who played piano, also left to pursue their education. With no one to play piano and help me, I lost interest and never played the violin again.

I was about nine when my Uncle Alvin invited me to spend the summer holidays on the farm. For the next 8 years, I spent every summer living with him and Aunt Annie. In 1937 a daughter, Elaine was born, and in 1946, Milton became the baby of the family. My Uncle became like a father to me. He taught me how to drive, run the farm machinery, and all about farming. He took me everywhere--sports days, ball games, Larson's Grove for picnics on Sundays. Wherever he went, I went. I was like one of the family. My Uncle farmed 6 quarters: 5 of his Dad's and one of his own. He had a Holt caterpillar and an Oliver 88 tractor. Seeding and summer fallowing were done with an eight-foot Cockshut oneway. When you pulled into a 160-acre field, it seemed as though it would take forever to get it seeded or plowed.

During those years there were some very good crops. Swathing was slow going as with the heavy crop we had to use the 12-foot swather. The canvas had seen better days, and one fall, the green straw would work under the canvas until it would jam, and before I could stop, the swather table was piled high with heavy, ripening wheat. Several times I had to clean off the table and it was heavy work. By late afternoon I was exhausted and when the canvas stopped again, I was so tired that before cleaning the table, I lay down on the wheat and went sound asleep. I awoke with my Uncle arriving in the truck. He helped me clear off the table, and I started the last round to finish the field. My Uncle had a fox terrier dog, called Trixie, and when I moved to the farm the dog and I became inseparable. Before harvest, I had taken a week off to spend some time with friends in Eston. I was told that while I was away, the dog just whined and howled, and wouldn't be consoled. What a welcome I received when I returned! Uncle Alvin had brought Trixie with him when he had come to the field to see why I was stopped. As I was going up the field, I saw my Uncle throwing stones at something, and I thought it was probably a gopher. When I finished the round, he told me he had had to kill Trixie; that the swather had cut off his legs. He had been completely hidden in the thick grain and hadn't been able to get out of the way when I started up. I bawled like a baby, and for the rest of the fall, tears weren't far away. How I missed that dog! I was 13 years old.

First Rambler Hockey Team
Back Row: Arnet Olson, Charlie McArthur (coach), Dr. Stewart Holmes, Wilbur Good, Bob Bertram, Lloyd Mytron, Judd Kraft, Russ Cambell
Front Row: Norm Mytron, Charlie Williams, Stan King, Cliff McIvor, Clement McCloskey

Chapter 4
A New Dad

A HANDSOME YOUNG MAN FROM IRELAND, JIMMY Hunter, an eligible bachelor, was an active member of the church. He was one of my Sunday School teachers. He had a job with the Eston Refinery and lived in a little shack on the grounds. He used to come to our home in the evenings and spent a lot of time with us kids; playing games, giving horseback rides, singing with us and for us. He had a deep baritone voice and he was ready with a song almost any time. He always sang as he worked. When I was 10, he and some friends planned a fishing trip to Jackfish Lake, and he took me along. We stayed in a tent and each evening, after supper, he would help by drying the dishes. He would sing one song after the other; Irish songs, hymns, comical songs, whatever came to mind. I heard voices outside the first night, and looking out, saw a crowd gathered beside the tent listening to him sing. Every night for the week we were there, he entertained the other campers.

Sometimes on the weekend, I would stay with him in his shack, and during the day, help him as he worked as a warehouse salesman at the Refinery. Later on, he even let me drive the big tanker trucks around in the yard. I had learned to drive at an early age from my Uncle Alvin, so really thought I was a big shot driving the big trucks. I even learned how to double-clutch! After playing with us kids in the evening, he would stay on after we were all in bed. Of course, I was curious to know what was going on, and would often listen at the bedroom door, but heard nothing. One night I got brave and came out of the bedroom to see what was happening. Mom quickly sprang from Jimmy's lap with a gasp, and I proceeded to the kitchen, saying I needed a drink. I knew then that they were serious.

On April 18, 1938, Mom and Jim were married. Four years later, Rhelda was born and two years later Stewart became part of the King-Hunter household. Jimmy was a brave man to marry a woman with three half-grown kids. My relationship with Jim changed dramatically after he moved in. I had always been envious of my friends who had Dads, but now I resented him taking the place of my Dad. As a larger house was needed, Mom and Jim bought an unfinished home and large property across the street from where we lived. The property was divided into lots and sold over the years, and the house was put on a full-sized basement and renovated from top to bottom. Jim moved a small barn onto the lot, bought a cow, and began selling milk. It was my job before school to tether the cow wherever there was grass, and after school, to move it to another area. In the winter I delivered milk with a sleigh. In those years, winters were much more severe with lots of snow and very cold temperatures. When warmer weather came, I delivered milk by bicycle. I acted miserable most of the time, would just grunt when spoken to, and let Jimmy know in no uncertain terms that I was not happy about doing anything for him. He was very patient and put up with a lot of my rebelliousness and never once raised his voice or spoke harshly to me. Eventually, he won me over and I began to call him Dad. He was as good a Dad as any biological father could be.

The Eston Refinery Company operated in Eston for six years, closing in 1941 due to WW2, as crude oil was no longer available for small refineries. Dad was out of work when the Refinery closed. As gas was rationed because of the war, Dad had a four-wheeled, horse-drawn, ply board van built and began delivering groceries for Central Department store. During the week, he could handle the deliveries, but it was another story on Saturdays. In the evening, the town would come alive. All the stores would remain open, the grocery store until midnight. Folks from the country would drive in to visit and to shop, and the streets would fill up with people. Deliveries were very heavy and I had to give Dad a hand. The movie theatre had two showings in the evening. When the first show was over, the townspeople would order their groceries and told us to set the groceries inside the door. Nobody locked the doors in those days. At 11:30 or later, the last show would end, and again, the people would rush in to shop. We had to try and deliver the groceries, so we didn't keep folks waiting up who wanted to get to bed. It was often 1:00 am before we would get home. Then we would have a little feast--whole wheat bread, jam, peanut butter, deli meats and other goodies. It was awfully hard to get out of bed Sunday morning to get to church on time for Sunday School!

King-Hunter Family Photo
L-R Ethel Hunter (Stan's Mom), Steve Gilkinson holding "Butch" (Steve Jr.), Joanne and Bess Gilkinson, unknown, Rhelda Hunter, Jim Hunter (Stan's Stepdad), Stewart Hunter, Stan holding Rhonnie, Phyl holding Michael, Thelma Pritchard holding Rod and Janice Pritchard

Chapter 5

MY LIFE WAS CHANGED

BEFORE THE TOWN OF ESTON BECAME A VILLAGE in 1916, the Methodists and Presbyterians were already holding meetings both in homes and Orange Hall. The Pentecostal message was spreading across the USA and Canada, and many churches were established throughout Saskatchewan. There was a hunger in the hearts of some of the Christians in Eston, who had heard of the Baptism of the Holy Spirit. Two Spirit-filled men from Texas, with the Assemblies of God, were holding evangelistic meetings in Manitoba. They felt led by the Lord to come to Eston, and in 1917, brought the Pentecostal message to the district. Several churches in Western Canada that had experienced the baptism of the Holy Spirit, and who had embraced the Eternal Security message. This is now known as the Grace Message, and it was strongly opposed by the Assemblies of God. Other doctrinal issues, such as the autonomy of the local church, led to like-minded churches forming a new fellowship entitled Full Gospel Missions. This later became the Evangelical Churches of Pentecost. Many young people being saved and filled with the Spirit. Many wanted to go into ministry, and many were called to the Mission Field. At a Full Gospel Missions conference in 1943, one of the main topics discussed was that of a Bible School. The eventual decision of the FGM was that a school should be built and that Eston should be the location.

In the fall of 1944, Full Gospel Bible Institute (FGBI) began with my pastor, Rev. Glen McLean as Principal; Wilf and Flo Marshall and Albert Marshall as resident faculty; and Ern Baxter and Lorne Pritchard as visiting faculty. The six, first-year students, later known as the Guinea Pigs, were billeted in homes. Classes were held in the basement and auditorium of the church. A few more students joined the others for the second semester. Although still not a Christian, I became good friends with all of the students. The fact that these young people would come here to spend months studying the Bible made a deep impression on me. Not all students went home over the Christmas season, and two ladies from Alberta, living in a light housekeeping suite, invited a friend and me to supper on New Year's Eve. It was evident that the purpose of the invitation was to share Christ with us. My friend and I had intended, after the meal, to go to the New Year's Eve dance. I was feeling the conviction of the Holy Spirit as we left, and when we arrived at the corner where the present Post Office is located, I stopped. To go to the dance we would turn right, and for me to go home I would turn left. I told my friend I was not able to go to the dance, said goodbye, and turned left. When I arrived home, I got down on my knees and made peace with God, by inviting Jesus into my life. From that moment on, my entire life was changed forever.

I knew a lot of the Old Testament stories and stories from the

Gospels from years of Sunday School and church, but I knew very little of the Christian life and spiritual growth. The problem was that a lot of our hockey games were played Wednesday and Friday evenings, the same evening as Bible Study and Prayer meeting at the church. I prayed the Lord would take away my love of hockey, but instead He gave me a greater love for Bible Study. I quit hockey, but it was not easy. We lived across the street from the rink, and I would come home after Bible Study or Prayer meeting and hear the roar of the crowd at the hockey game, awakening my passion for the game.

The Pastor asked if I would give leadership to the Young People's Meetings. I hesitated because I had always been a shy kid, and terrified of taking any public part in anything. I didn't mind too much leading the singing, organizing activities, or working behind the scenes, but the thought of having to pray or preach in public was intimidating. However, I knew I was going to have to give it a try if I wanted to grow and develop spiritually. I accepted, but the experience showed me I was no preacher! I invited Jack Northcott, a student from the nearby village of Snipe Lake, to help me. We involved the students as much as we could, and I did my best with the preaching with very short messages. Thanks to the goodness of the Lord, the Young Peoples grew spiritually as well as numerically.

The Principal of the public school had recommended me to the local Central Department Store for a job in the hardware department. I worked there until the end of the school year, then went to work for the last time with my Uncle Alvin. Granddad Shuttleworth came from Vancouver every fall. After harvest, he asked if I was interested in farming. If so, he would help me get land and get set up. As much as I loved farming, I knew the Lord had other things for me, so I had to decline. That summer, I joined several others from the church and was baptized by immersion in the Name of the Lord Jesus Christ near Lancer ferry in the South Saskatchewan River.

In September of 1945, I enrolled in FGBI. There were lots of activities at the school. I joined the choir, sang in a trio and a quartet, went to surrounding towns for children's Happy Hour, and joined a prayer band. Not long after classes began, I joined three other fellows several nights a week for prayer, for sharing and seeking the Lord's direction in our lives. I was very interested in Missions and read all the books on missionaries' lives I could get my hands on. The three that impressed me the most were two written by Rosalind Goforth, "Goforth of China" and "How I know... God Answers Prayer" and I can't remember the Author of the third, "Mary Slessor of Calabar."

The student body was divided into prayer bands, each praying for a different country or region. I chose the Africa band, as it had fewer students involved even though I had no real interest in Africa. I was more interested in China because of the books I had read and in India because of the missionaries who had visited the church over the years. All through that first year, I kept asking the Lord where He would have me serve as a missionary, but I got no direct answer to my prayers. The more I prayed the more the Lord seemed to be saying to be patient, that the answer would come, and that I would know because it would be a place of great need. I thought to myself, how would I know because where isn't there a great need? Soon after Bible School began, the Davies brothers from Vancouver visited the church. Martin and Alice Davies had served many years in West Africa and Phyl and Lucille were on their way for the first time. They said they planned to start a new Mission in Upper Volta, West Africa. I was impressed with their presentation, but being very shy, I never talked with them. Little did I realize the important role these two couples would later play in my life.

During the summer, I teamed up with another student, Art Sheppard, to do some tent evangelism. We were invited to Luseland by a Christian family, but as no unbelievers came, it turned out to be a 10 day camp for Christians. From there we moved to the Alcock farm near Kerrobert. We lived with them and had meetings in their living room. The move and the location were certainly God's timing, as people came from the town and countryside, and several came to know Christ as Saviour. We ended the rally with a weekend camp meeting in the tent pitched in the yard to accommodate the crowds. Rev. Lorne Pritchard was the camp speaker. It was the beginning of the Kerrobert church that over the years served the town and community well.

I returned to FGBI for the 1946-47 term. I was still waiting to know where the Lord was preparing me to serve. Soon after arriving in Africa, the Davies applied to the Federation of Protestant Missions in French West Africa to begin a new mission in an area that had several smaller tribes that were not being evangelized. While waiting on permission, they went to Leo, the Administrative Centre of the area, to confer with the French Commander. He permitted them to choose a site, and later to build temporary houses. They were also permitted to begin the principal purpose of the Mission—to preach the Gospel. Phyl Davies wrote a letter to Rev. McLean that was read in a Sunday morning service. In the letter, he wrote that when approved, the Mission would be responsible for a large area in the south-west part of the country and that they would need all the missionaries who could come to Upper Volta for many, many years to come. As soon as that sentence was read, it felt like I was hit in the chest by a bolt of lightning. God witnessed to my spirit at that moment that this was the place of great need that He had spoken of the year before and that He had told me I would recognize when it was made known. The pastor had chosen a missionary song, "I'll Go Where You Want Me to go," to sing after the reading of the letter, and invited different students to sing a verse. The congregation joined in on the chorus. He called my name to sing the third verse, but I was trembling so much inside by what had just transpired that I couldn't sing through the verse, as the reality of the words I was singing struck home.

> There's surely somewhere a lowly place,
> In earth's harvest fields so white
> Where I may labour through life's short day
> For Jesus, the Crucified.
> So, trusting my all to Thy tender care
> And knowing Thou lovest me
> I'll do Thy will with a heart sincere
> And be what You want me to be.

Stan (2nd from far right) and Art (far right)

FGBI Students 1946

At the end of the chorus, still trembling, I told the congregation what had just transpired. Not only had the Lord revealed the country to which I was being sent, but also the very location. Sometime later, I made an appointment to talk with my Pastor. The result of that talk was certainly not what I expected it to be. As diplomatically as he could, he told me that he did not think I was missionary material. Knowing my shyness, and difficulty speaking in public, he reminded me that missionaries had to do a lot of preaching. He suggested that because the new venture in Africa would need a lot of prayer, and financial support, I could fulfill what the Lord had laid on my heart by getting a good job and supporting the venture financially and by prayer. Much later, I realized this was all the Lord's doing; a test of my faith in preparation for my ministry in Africa. How miserably I failed that first real test.

Thelma, Stan, unknown

Chapter 6
TRYING TO FORGET GOD

NEEDLESS TO SAY, I WAS STUNNED AND PERPLEXED by my Pastor's reaction. I knew it would be impossible to get to the Mission Field without his and the church's support. I had to agree with the Pastor that my preaching was worse than terrible, but I thought maybe I could be useful in other ways and free up someone else to do more preaching. Was all that the Lord had seemed to be talking to me about missions just my imagination? I was most sincere when I told the Lord that I would serve Him on a mission field anywhere. Was the Lord mocking me? A thousand questions filled my thoughts. I was so confused; I didn't know where or to whom I could turn. In the spring a friend invited me to drive to Vancouver with him where he was going to look for work. I thought that if all I was good for was to get a job, why did I need more Bible School? I would go to the Coast, look for a job and forget about the mission field. I stayed with my Grandma Shuttleworth and soon found a job at Burns Meat Packing Plant. A few months later, through a friend of my Uncle Dave, I got a job as a deck-hand on Lady Cynthia with the Union Steamship Company. We carried passengers, food, cargo and mail up Howe Sound and the Sunshine Coast. Sorry to say I was angry with God, stopped reading my Bible, praying and going to church. However, I soon learned the Lord was not through with me yet. I had an accident on the dock at one port and tore the cartilage in my right knee and ended up in City Hospital for an operation to remove the torn section. Lying on my back in the hospital with my leg in a cast, unable to get out of bed, I did a lot of thinking, and the Lord did a lot of talking in my heart. I was surprised to have a visit from Wilf and Florence Marshall; teachers at FGBI. They were God's emissaries and talked about the Lord, my call to the mission field, and they brought me some Christian literature to read. Before I left the hospital I had repented of my waywardness and turned my life back over to the Lord.

In three weeks, I was able to start back to work on The Cynthia. Christmas Eve, we were scheduled to return to Vancouver around midnight. To make our next port, we had to sail north to get around a mile-long reef. Sometime later, I learned that the 1st mate, wanting to get home earlier, decided to try to cross the reef at a point where he knew there was a break. I was on deck watching the waves break over the reef, looking for the opening toward which the ship was supposedly heading. Just as I leaned over the rail, we struck the rock, almost caving in my chest against the rail. The front end of the Cynthia had been reinforced and used to ram submarines during the war, so the bow of the ship slid up the reef and settled down past the reinforcing, forming a sort of ball and socket. We tried lowering the two lifeboats on board, but the ropes had rotted and the pulleys were frozen; they were left dangling. We were able to lower a skiff but had trouble getting into it as the rope ladders were also in poor condition. Six of us moved it over the reef and rowed to a small community on the Island to deliver the mail. A ship came to take all but one of the officers back to Vancouver. Christmas Day we heard on the radio news that Union Steamship Company had not forgotten the crew on board, but that turkey dinner with all the trimmings had been sent. We, on board, didn't know where it had been delivered, but it certainly never arrived at the Cynthia! I volunteered to remain on board as part of a skeleton crew. For the next several days, tugs tried to move the ship off the reef, but even at high tide, it refused to budge. The sister ship, the Cecilia, was sent out to help tow, but the swell caused by the Cecilia, as it swung past the stern of the Cynthia, was sufficient to lift the bow, allowing the tugs to pull it free. The ship was towed by tug to the dry dock in Vancouver. I was allowed to sleep on board that night, was paid the next day, and was then out of a job. The Union Steamship Company went out of business a short time later.

I was attending Evangelistic Tabernacle at the time. The church had recently purchased the St. Giles United Church, and I volunteered to help with the renovations being done before the congregation moved in. Not able to find a job in the Vancouver area, I moved back to Eston, planning to return to Bible School in the fall. My sister, Thelma, had recently married Les Pritchard, and, as they were considering going as missionaries to India, they had enrolled in the Missionary Medical Institute, later renamed Health Institute, in Toronto. They invited me to join them.

When crossing the border into the USA, apparently, for some

reason, Les had not received the proper documentation. We were almost refused entry back into Canada when we arrived at Sault Ste. Marie, as Les had no papers to prove he had not bought the car in the States. Thelma and I were praying while Les was dealing with the Authorities, and, eventually, we were allowed to enter. The forests in Northern Ontario were breathtaking with the leaves turning into their brilliant fall colors, and the maple leaves were almost as large as dinner plates. It was a spectacular drive until we arrived in the Toronto area.

Les & Thelma Pritchard, Stan

Chapter 7
FURTHER PREPARATIONS

ALTHOUGH I HAD NOT PRE-REGISTERED AT THE school, I had been accepted as a student. I slept in one of the extra classrooms until Les and Thelma moved into a newly purchased house trailer. I moved in with them until I was able to get a job at Eaton's Department Store and find a room in a private rooming house. A twenty-minute bus ride took me to the Institute in the morning for classes. The afternoon was free unless you were scheduled for some practical duty in the Senior's Hospital on the grounds. All of the students had to spend some time on the wards. My duties included making beds, bathing male patients, giving enemas and cleaning wards.

After Christmas, another student and I were the first to observe hospital life for a month at Toronto Western Hospital. We spent the first two weeks in the pharmacy, observing and helping fill the requisitions that came from different floors. I felt some apprehension one morning as I filled a request for a certain pill. A .5 gr. pill was asked for, but a short while later a nurse came with the pills and wanted to verify the strength, as the pills were much larger than usual. I immediately knew I had made the mistake in strength; had sent a 1.5 gr. instead, and only the alertness of the nurse had prevented patients from getting a much larger dose than prescribed.

We also helped make up a batch of Calamine lotion, an anti-itching treatment for adults with rashes, such as poison ivy, measles, or sunburn, and it was my job to pour it into a larger container. Later on, when the pharmacist went for some Calamine lotion, he found the container empty. We soon discovered that I had poured the lotion in with the Calamine cream, used for diaper rash and child skincare. The assistant pharmacist said she should be angry with me for the mistake. But, because on a test she had given us she had marked a mathematical question wrong that I had been able to show her was right, she said she would say nothing. I told her I deserved to be reprimanded as I had been told over and over again, in the pharmacy everything was to be checked at least twice. I realized that dispensing medicine is a very exact occupation where there is no room for error.

While some surgeons wouldn't allow us in the operating room, others did. We received anatomy lessons as the surgeon showed us different organs through the incision he had made. We followed the nurses as they made their rounds, and Doctors and interns as they went from bed to bed discussing the patients' illnesses and medications. The latter didn't do us much good as we didn't always understand the medical terminology.

To me, the most interesting experiences were the two visits made to the morgue. The one autopsy was on a pharmacist, a heavy smoker, who had died from lung cancer. As the cancer had metastasized, all the organs had to be examined to see how far the cancer had spread. The doctor asked if I would assist him, and as he removed the various organs, he had me weigh them and place them on a table to be dissected later. It was so interesting to see a brain, a heart, a liver, and a kidney and hold them in my hands. His lungs were completely black, stuck to the chest cavity, and had to be literally torn free. The second autopsy was to determine the cause of death of an elderly lady. It was an almost surreal experience, as at the time, I had no sense the organs I was handling were from real people who had been alive just a short while before.

One Saturday an intern, a brother in Christ, asked if I would scrub and help him with a finger amputation he had to do in an emergency. It bothered me more to see the amputated finger lying on the tray than what I had observed in the morgue. We returned to classes for the remaining month and had some catching up to do because of the classes we had missed while at the Hospital. On May 26, 1949, I graduated from Missionary Health Institute with an award in Tropical Medicine.

While at the Health Institute I had heard of an orphanage opened in Quebec by a Christian Dutch couple, the Vandervalks. They were asking for volunteers. Thinking it a good way to do something helpful, and at the same time learn French, I volunteered. I returned to Eston for a short visit, taking time to talk of my plans again with my Pastor. He saw that I was determined to prepare for the mission field, and willingly gave his blessing. I returned east by railway, as ordained ministers received a book of coupons giving a discount on fares.

While waiting for a connection in Detroit, I took the time to attend a Detroit Tigers baseball game. I was the only one in the far-right bleachers, when the Bakers, from Idaho, who had also been students at MHI, sat in the same row. What would be the odds of such a meeting in Detroit, at a baseball park seating 90 thousand spectators, two weeks after leaving MHI?

In Toronto, I moved into a room in the home where I had stayed while attending classes. I met up with a friend, Stuart Wilson, who had also been at MHI. He was pastoring a small church while working for his Dad, who had recently moved to Toronto from the United States as CEO of Dempster's Bakery. I had the opportunity to share the Word with his congregation, and travel with him as he delivered Dempster's bread and baked goods to smaller towns around the area.

I attended People's Church Sunday morning and was surprised and happy to run into Jerry Marquis who had also been a student at MHI. As she had become good friends with Marg Wright, and Marg and Stu were in a relationship, we had all been together at times. Jerry and I spent the rest of the day together. One evening, I received a phone call from Eldon and Luella Johnson, classmates at FGBI, who had also felt the call of God to Upper Volta. They had been accepted as candidates and were on their way to Montreal to learn French. They had phoned to see if I would like a ride to Montreal, on my way to the orphanage.

I took the bus from Montreal to the small town of Bondville, where I was met by Swede, a Swedish immigrant who was working at the orphanage. The Vandervalks had been able to purchase two small adjacent farms; one farmhouse becoming the boys' home and the other, the girls'. Two ladies were also working at the orphanage: one, a schoolteacher, and the other helping in the kitchen as well as caring for the small children. All the children ate together, often outdoors when the weather permitted.

I soon learned that each day would begin by rounding up cattle from the pasture for milking at 5:00 am, separating the milk, putting the cream cans out to be collected, and grooming the horses—all before breakfast. The rest of the day varied according to what needed to be done on the farm. Water had to be pumped twice daily for the horses and cows, there was an early and late hay crop to be mowed and stacked, an oat crop to be cut and put through the hammer mill as feed for the cattle, a field or two to be plowed, and repair jobs to be done around the farms.

Brother Vandervalk had a great garden, part of which, with help from some of the older boys and girls, I peddled from cottage to cottage around near-by Brome Lake. Sundays I helped with Sunday School and sometimes spoke at the morning service. After supper and after the cows and horses had been cared for, I generally had a fun time with the boys, waiting for Sister Vandervalk to be free for my French lesson. It was all I could do to keep my eyes open, let alone learn French. When I arrived in May, none of the kids spoke English, and I spoke no French. When I left in December, all the kids spoke English while I had learned very little French! However, I did learn a lot about kids, which helped immensely later on in Africa. I realized later that I had been too strict with the boys, punishing them for small misdemeanors instead of taking time to talk to them, like most fathers would. I know by the time I left, some of those kids had more problems than I had helped them with.

I did take a break for one week. My friend, Stu Wilson, wrote to let me know he was planning a trip to visit his lady friend, Marg. Marg had invited Jerry to come too, and they were wondering if I would be able to join them. I had become very fond of Jerry, and I knew she had some feelings for me, so I decided to join them. I hitchhiked to Montreal, took a city bus as far as it would go, and then hitchhiked to Toronto.

The four of us piled into a coupe, to make the three-hour drive north to Marg's home. Marg's parents were very gracious, fed us well, and left us very much to ourselves. To leave Stu and Marg alone as much as we could, Jerry and I did a lot of walking and talking by ourselves. Stu had to leave early because of his job, and 3 days later Marg also had to return to Toronto for her job. It was my pleasure to drive the two ladies in Marg's coupe. It was very difficult to say goodbye to Jerry. I was too timid to express my feelings for her, and maybe she was waiting for me to say something. As it was, we parted with just a handshake and thank-yous for the wonderful time. I never saw Jerry again although for the next year and a half we corresponded regularly.

Chapter 8
BACK TO BIBLE SCHOOL

I LEFT THE HOME FOR MONTREAL AT THE END OF November, got a job at Eaton's Department store, and stayed with another friend from MHI. As my French was not good enough to work in the sales department, I was assigned to parcel wrapping. I volunteered for overtime work so that I would make more money to purchase things I would need for Africa, such as sheets and towels and some clothing, while still eligible for the staff discount.

The week before Christmas, on my way home to Eston, I spent a few days with my sister, Thelma, and her husband, Les, who were pastoring a church in Winnipeg at the time. The prairies were experiencing a severe cold spell, and when it was time to leave for the train station, Les was unable to start his car. He phoned every taxi company in the phone book, all of which were booked up solidly. He finally persuaded one company to send a taxi to get me to the station before the train left. It was too late to check my baggage through, and because of the shopping I had done in Eaton's, I had a lot of baggage to take on board with me. The baggage master was not happy at all, but I finally persuaded him to check all my suitcases through to Saskatoon. I arrived home to Eston the day before Christmas.

I enrolled at FGBI for the second semester. In the spring, Martin and Alice Davies, who recently arrived in Canada from Upper Volta, spoke at the church and to the students at the school. They were able to confirm that the Upper Volta Mission was now officially recognized by the Government and there was room for many more missionaries. Martin told of an experience he had recently had on the Field that the Lord used to jolt my heart again. He had been awakened on a moonlit night by a voice in a native language crying out in the nearby bush. He woke his brother, Phyl, and a native Christian, and together they made their way through the bush until they came to a clearing. There they saw a young man kneeling on the ground in front of a sacred rock, crying out, over and over, "Give me life! Give me life!" I knew that the young man represented thousands of people in the area for which the Upper Volta Mission was now responsible. The only hope for these people was the Gospel, and I was challenged again to be one of those who would take this message of hope.

I spoke to Martin after the service and together we talked with my Pastor. The outcome of that meeting was that the church would support me monthly while in France learning the French language, and for the first three-year term on the Field. Alice Davies wrote a letter in French to enroll me in a language school in Paris. She also wrote a letter for a young lady from New Westminster, BC; Phyllis Burr, a former student at FGBI and later, a member of the teaching staff who had already been approved as a schoolteacher for the

Mission kids in Upper Volta.

In a short while, confirmation was received from the School in Paris. The hardest part for me now, because of my dread of preaching, was to share my vision with the churches across the prairies and raise funds for the equipment I would need. Passage to England had to be booked immediately. It was 1950; a year of Jubilee for the Catholic Church, and every ship sailing out of Canada and the States for Europe was booked solid. The CN Railway Station Agent persevered and finally was able to reserve space for me on a ship, the Samaria. To help meet the need for more passenger space, Cunard Lines had recommissioned the ship, which had been used during the war as a troop carrier. I phoned Phyllis and was happy to hear that her brother, an employee of a Steamship Company in Vancouver, had been able to book her passage on the same boat.

The Pastors and their congregations were very gracious, and I received prayer support and sufficient funds to purchase more of the essential things I would need in Africa. Many friends and members of the Eston church provided numerous items until I had a good assortment of small tools, kitchen supplies, bedroom necessities, and clothes. They all had to be packed in crates, trunks and barrels and stored in my family's basement, awaiting shipping. I think many in the church were just as excited about me going to Africa as a Missionary as I was.

Chapter 9

GOODBYE, CANADA

SAYING GOODBYE TO FAMILY AND FRIENDS WAS much easier than I had thought it might be. Everyone was happy for me, knowing how much I was looking forward to beginning life in Africa. To Mom, four years or more seemed like a long time, and naturally, she was apprehensive as she knew somewhat of the dangers I would face. Africa was still called the Dark Continent, and West Africa still called the White Man's Grave because of malaria. Mom was a very quiet person but with strong faith, and I knew she would be praying for me. Dad and I loaded my suitcases in the car, he and my Pastor prayed, then Dad and I headed for Swift Current where I caught the CPR train.

The Samaria was to sail from Quebec City, and the cheapest way there was by train across the northern States. The Railways issued coupon books that reduced fares for ordained ministers. On the way, I stopped in Chicago for a visit with my great Aunt and her two daughters. I also got in touch with Phyllis who I knew was in the city visiting her Uncle and family. Phyllis took a direct train from Chicago to Quebec City while I went via New York to check a missionary wholesale place about some equipment I might need at a later date. I booked into the landmark Le Chateau Frontenac Hotel in the old city. Phyl was staying with a friend but during the next few days, we did considerable sight-seeing together. One of the most interesting sites we visited was the Plains of Abraham. It was here that General Wolfe and the British army defeated General Montcalm and the French army in 1759, resulting in Canada becoming a British Colony.

On August 15, 1950, the Samaria sailed out of Quebec City for Liverpool, England. As the Samaria had been a troop carrier during the war, below deck was like a large dormitory with rows of double bunk beds where the men were accommodated. The women occupied what had been the officers' staterooms on the main deck; three ladies to a room. As most of the men stayed below deck to visit, play cards, smoke and chew tobacco, the air was always heavy with smoke and body odour. Phyllis and I got deck chairs as the weather was ideal for the nine days we spent at sea, so I spent all my waking time out on deck.

Before we left the Gulf of St. Lawrence, we ran into heavy fog, and for an hour or two had to listen to the foghorn blasting. After passing through the Strait of Belle Isle and starting to cross the Atlantic, the days became cooler and there was quite a swell, which kept some people out of the dining room for a few meals. Phyllis missed one or two until she got more accustomed to the ship's rolling motion. We awoke one morning to a beautiful yet chilling sight; a large, green and blue iceberg shimmering in the morning sunlight. Shortly afterward, we witnessed another spectacular sight in the distance; a pod of whales was rolling, splashing and spouting as they frolicked about.

Upon arrival, the Samaria anchored outside of Liverpool because of low tide and we had to spend the night on board. The next morning a boat train took us to St. Pancras station in London. While in London, we had made reservations to stay at the headquarters of Worldwide Evangelization Crusade, WEC, a British Missions Society. It was such a joy to meet the Director of WEC, Norman Grubb, son-in-law of C. T. Studd, the founder of the Mission. We also met many veteran missionaries from several different countries, and others, like ourselves, who were missionary candidates. Morning devotions, led by Brother Grubb or a missionary from some foreign country, were deep spiritual blessings, and challenges as well. On Sunday we went to Westminster Chapel to hear Dr. Graham Scroggie, a renowned Bible teacher, and Author. As his books were used so much at FGBI, it was a real pleasure to hear him in person.

We soon found it is impossible to see London in just a few days. It was like being in a living history book. We spent most of our days walking to some of the nearby sights in London such as Buckingham Palace, Westminster Abbey, the Houses of Parliament, St. Paul's Cathedral, the Tower of London, and taking bus tours to visit others, such as Madame Tussauds. Everywhere we went there was evidence of the war. Here and there, among buildings that showed where they had been patched and repaired, there was only the shell of a former building and a pile of rubble. It was remarkable, though, to see the work that had been done to repair the damage done by the war.

We did get to see some of rural England. On the boat, we met a young couple, Mel and Sylvia Quick, from Alberta, who were going to spend a year or so living with Sylvia's family in England while they prepared for missionary work in Peru. They invited us to visit them in Bognor Regis, a lovely modern resort which was built in the 1780s as the first English seaside resort developed for bathing. Many wealthy people came for health and relaxation to the reportedly healthy saltwater there, including King George V in 1928. He came to convalesce after a serious illness, and so it was given the title "Regis" (of the King). The two-hour train ride there took us through the countryside that was beautiful with lush, green meadows and luxurious dark green trees. Here and there on winding roads were quaint, thatched-roofed houses nestled in the trees, and a few small villages, one with the impressive Arundel Castle. Built in 1067, it has been the home of the Dukes of Norfolk for the last 400 years.

The following day the Quicks took us by bus to Chichester, the oldest Roman town in Britain. In 43 AD the Romans invaded Britain and soon built a fort on the townsite. Some of the Roman remains still to be seen are the largest Roman palace in Britain built during the first century, the original defensive ditches that encircled the city, the bathhouses, and the site of an 800 seat Amphitheater, built around 80 AD, where gladiators fought to the death.

Chapter 10
Gai Paree

WE TOOK A BUS BACK TO LONDON IN THE EVENING and spent the next day resting and getting packed, ready to leave for Paris the following morning. There is what is called a boat-train, where the train crosses on a ferry and passengers remain on the train from London to Paris. Unfortunately, it was completely booked, so we had to settle for a train to Newhaven, a ferry across the Channel to Dieppe, and another train to Paris. It was a long, tiresome trip, mainly because of the number of people travelling. We found one seat on the train while many passengers were left standing. We sat on our suitcases on the ferry and were grateful that the crossing was smooth.

At Dieppe, we had to run from the boat to the train to get a seat. I'm sure it was God's timing that we had met a young Australian man in Pancras Station in London who stayed with us all the way to Paris. He was a wonderful help as he knew a significant amount of French. I'm sure the three of us made quite a picture running down the dock to the train at Dieppe. It was raining for one thing, and as the dock was wet, we had to be careful not to slip, while we were each one bowed down with luggage.

    Phyllis and I had checked through most of our belongings, keeping only what we thought we would need until we found lodging in Paris, but even so, we each had a heavy suitcase and a typewriter, as well as our coats and Phyllis' hatbox and umbrella. We wore the coats and I carried the two suitcases while Phyllis carried the typewriters; our friend juggled the other things along with his luggage. We made the train, and thanks to our Australian friend, who tipped the porter, we did get seats—and what seats they were! They were hard and narrow, the backs were bolt upright, and there were two of us to a seat. We were almost as comfortable as when we were sitting on our suitcases!

    We were about nine hours from London to Paris and were exhausted when we arrived at Saint-Lazar station, in the early evening, in a strange place, not knowing the language, and having no place to stay. There were hundreds of passengers milling around the station, either arriving or leaving on trains. Thankfully, our friend stayed with us and eventually, after finding a porter who said he would look after us, we said goodbye and our Australian friend disappeared into the crowd.

    I phoned the school to see what accommodation they had for us, but the person on the other end could not speak a word of English. As I tried to explain what I was asking, she got more and more agitated and finally slammed down the receiver.

    Again, we sat on our luggage until the porter brought over a man wearing a dirty, worn trench coat and a felt hat, who beckoned us to follow him. As the man made no effort to help with our luggage, we gathered it up and tagged along after him as best we could. He led us out into the rain, down one narrow street after another, stopping now and then to allow us to catch up. It was dark and damp and we had no idea where we were going. We began to doubt the wisdom of following this man, but eventually, arrived at a small hotel. It looked as though it might have been a private home at one time. I had cashed a Traveler's Cheque at the station but had no idea of the value of any of the French money. I pulled out one of the bills and handed it to the man. He took it, then reached over and took a larger denomination out of my hand and disappeared out the door.

Chapter 11
ALLIANCE FRANCAISE

The Hotel was clean, neat and very comfortable. After breakfast, which was served in our rooms, we took a bus to the school—Alliance Francaise. After talking to several different people, I was to understand the school did not provide lodging. However, we were given a list of names and addresses of people who had rooms to rent. We registered, paid one month's tuition, and were sent to the 2nd floor. A tiny, middle-aged lady was sitting at a desk in front of a line-up of prospective students, talking excitedly in French, and gesticulating widely with both arms, to the students. We found out when it was our turn that all the students had to write down as best they could a short dictation read by this lady. She would correct it and, accordingly, would assign each student to the class level they would begin. Phyllis was assigned to the second Beginners' class, and I, a more advanced class. I chose to start in the second class as well, as I wanted the best foundation possible.

We spent all day finding our way by bus or by the metro (subway) from one address to the next. Bus and Metro travel is quite easy in

Paris as the routes are very clearly marked. But, after riding miles, walking up and down streets, climbing stairs, trying to make ourselves understood, and trying to understand, we found nothing that suited either one of us. We returned to the same hotel for the night. On the way, Phyllis asked me if there was a low convenience with a stopper and water taps in my bathroom. There was, so we discussed what it could be, and concluded that it was probably a foot bath. It wasn't until much later during our stay in France that we learned it is called a bidet, which means "a riding pony" and is used for intimate hygiene!

The following day we started the search again and of all the places we visited, only one was promising. It was a beautiful two-story home on a short, quiet and pretty street in Boulogne, a suburb of Paris, and just a five-minute walk to the Bois de Boulogne, a beautiful park built around a man-made lake. It was a little more expensive than others, but there were two separate bedrooms, and both noon and evening meals were included. The owner, Madame Vexiau, a widow, lived on the main floor, and her son, his wife, and their three children on the second floor. When we mentioned that the rent was more than we could pay, she reduced it, as she said she would like us to stay. She was so pleased we were from Canada. We learned later that the French were incredibly grateful for Canada's part in the liberation of France toward the end of the war.

We had about a 10-minute walk to the Metro, a 30-minute ride underground, and another short walk to the School. Alliance is a very large school with students from all over the world. At that time, shortly after the war, the city of Paris was full of American GIs, much to the chagrin of the Parisians. They resented the late entry of the States in the war, and after the war, the continual bragging about winning the war. With the number of GIs enrolled, it seemed that every class was over half American. Consequently, the classes were rather large. Regular classes were in the mornings from 9:00 until noon. I found all the teachers to be particularly good, but there wasn't much time given for interaction. The classes were mostly grammar and spelling, with little time for conversation.

However, two afternoons a week, there were special advanced classes for pronunciation and conversation with fewer students. The Instructors were professors from the University. We nicknamed the lady prof "Madam Butterfly". She was ever elegantly dressed and always wore a large hat and flowing silk scarf around her neck. As she waltzed into the room, she would be loudly repeating the pronunciation of the French vowels, the ends of the scarf fluttering out behind her. The male prof emphasized conversation and comprehension. Phyl got some extra help from one of her lady professors who also taught English. Once a week, Phyl would give her an hour of English and she would give Phyl an hour of French.

There were many Christian students attending the school, most of them preparing for missionary work in some French-speaking colony. Permission had been granted for us to meet once a week in one of the classrooms for a time of fellowship, sharing and prayer. Different ones were asked to bring a message from the Word. Eventually, the time came when I was asked. I wanted to refuse, and yet, well aware of my lack of speaking ability, I somehow consented, but with fear and trembling. On that fateful day, I surprised even myself at the composure and the fluency I had in sharing from John Chapter six and even received many thanks from the other students. I know that it was only the Holy Spirit that had enabled me, but it gave me hope that, after all, I might have a preaching ministry in Africa.

Chapter 12
LIFE AT MADAME VEXIAU'S

LIFE AT MADAME VEXIAU'S WAS INTERESTING, TO say the least. The meals were incredible with lunch served at noon, or as soon as we got back from classes. Dinner was at 8:00 pm. and served one course at a time; soup, a meat dish, a vegetable, a second vegetable and all eaten with pieces of bread broken off of a long narrow French baguette. Finally, dessert was served, most often fresh fruit or a variety of cheeses, and quite often, a pastry. In the evenings I often sat in the living room to visit with Madame while she knit. As she spoke a bit of English, she was a great help to me with my French. She suggested I read to her and over the following months, I read several interesting French books. I am sure it must have been hard for her to listen to my fractured French, but evening after evening she listened, helping me with pronunciation and vocabulary. Before long I was reading quite fluently and understanding much more, thanks in large part to Madame Vexiau.

Winters in Paris can be quite cold and wet. The central heating was only turned on in the evenings of the coldest days, and even then, we had to wear extra clothing. Even though we were charged for using our space heaters, we had no choice but to use them during afternoons and weekends we were home to supplement the heat from the central heating. The summer weather proved to be very warm with some days exceptionally hot, whereas the spring and fall were beautiful.

My room opened through two glass doors onto a large backyard with lovely flower beds, a few trees, and a beautiful lawn where I spent much of my time studying. I used to leave one of the doors open with the drape pulled back during the hot nights. One night I was awakened by the drape being jerked back through the open door. I let out a yell loud enough to wake the dead, and the drape dropped down. I ran to the door just in time to see in the moonlight a man scale up and over the wall surrounding the backyard. Madame Vexiau said it was not safe to leave anything, not even a small bathroom window, open at night because of thieves circulating in the neighborhood.

On many weekends Phyl and I would go exploring the sights of Paris and the surrounding area. Like London, Paris cannot be seen in only a few days, but unlike London, we had much more time to visit interesting places. The Eiffel Tower, the tallest structure in Europe, the Louvre with the famous Mona Lisa and Michelangelo's statue of the body of Jesus in the lap of Mary, the Champs Elysses, one of the most beautiful, luxurious and expensive streets in the world, the Arc de Triomphe with the tomb of the unknown soldier, Versailles, the palace of the Kings, Malmaison, the home of Josephine, Napoleon's wife and, later Napoleon's as well, Notre Dame on Christmas Eve; these among many, many others, were well worth a visit.

    We found a church to our liking within walking distance of our home. The Pastor, Rev. Roberts, was a missionary to France with the Welsh Apostolic Church. In the Sunday morning worship service, there was lovely liberty in the Spirit and often a prophetic word or message in tongues. Communion was served every Sunday. The 5:00 service was open to testimonies and ended with a time of prayer for the sick and other needs. During the week there was a Bible Study and a Children's Meeting. Phyl was asked to teach some classes on Child Evangelism, and to do some children's work in the summer.

    About an hour's metro ride and a 15-minute walk away was a very large Assemblies of God church. The Allcocks and Brother Owen, friends of the Burr family, were having meetings in several European cities. While in Paris, Phyllis, of course, wanted to attend and I was glad to accompany her. Their meetings were well attended, and many responded to the Gospel and the teaching of the Word, and many were healed. We enjoyed our time with them on Sundays, and during the week when they came to visit us at Madame Vexiau's.

    The next stops for the Allcocks were Luxemburg and Belgium, and they invited Phyllis and I to come along for the ride. It was nice to get a break from classes and to visit two other countries. In the countryside we drove past farm after farm with grass-roofed houses and with the animal barn attached to the house. I'm sure it was handy to have the barn so close, but I'm not sure the smell was always delightful! Back in Paris, it was back to the books again.

Stan, Sis Roberts, Phyllis, Bro Roberts, Madame Vexiau, Jim Riccitelli

Chapter 13
ADJUSTING

PHYLLIS AND I HAD ALWAYS GOTTEN ALONG VERY well, and we had a lot of fun along the way. We had become good friends while at FGBI and later, whenever Phyllis came back to Eston, my Mom would invite her over. As we had both been called to Africa around the same time, we kept in touch to know how things were progressing in our plans. I was very happy when everything had fallen into place for us to travel together on our way to France. Years later I know she felt the same way, as she had written to her mother, "Yes Mother, I do thank the Lord for Stan...It would not have been at all practical for me to have come to this land (France) and to England alone. We get along fine together, but I do not expect anything permanent will come of it. We are really like a brother and sister. I feel too, that there is too much difference in our ages."

However, once we got into the routine of classes, our relationship changed. I know Phyllis found my nature difficult at times and there were things in her nature that were difficult for me. I have never been a great conversationalist, and as I have problems expressing myself, I find it hard to take part in conversations. Phyllis, on the other hand, loved to talk and had no trouble carrying on a conversation with anyone. When we were continually on the move and seeing new things all the time, conversation became easier. But as we were together so much, walking or riding the underground day after day, I found little to talk about. I know she thought I was moody when I didn't feel like talking which resulted in our relationship being strained at times. One of Phyl's habits in particular really bothered me—she was almost always late. At FGBI she received the pseudonym "the late Miss Burr". As I have always thought it important to be on time, it was very frustrating to me to be late so much of the time.

One of the hardest trials on the mission field is to learn to get along with fellow missionaries. The oppressive heat, the isolation, the loneliness, dealing with people of a different culture and other adjustments tend, at times, to bring out the worst in one's nature. We had to learn more than just French while in France. I believe the Lord was using our close relationship to teach us how to adjust to one other and later, to those with whom we would be working on the mission field. It was necessary to learn to let the fruit of the Spirit predominate in every situation.

At the same time, I was struggling with another problem. As I was not a romantic, I found it difficult to start and maintain a relationship with those of the opposite sex. I had wanted to on at least three different occasions—a student at FGBI, with Jerry, the American student at MHI, and a Norwegian girl in my class at Alliance. But because of my shyness and lack of self-confidence, these young ladies moved on and out of my life, without knowing how much I cared for them. Now, because of our friendship, and because we were together so much, I was fighting my feelings toward Phyllis which had gone beyond friendship. One reason I was holding back was that she was older than was I. Then too, I did not want Phyllis to know my feelings for her, as I did not know what her reaction would be. However, a few days before Christmas we found ourselves alone as Madame Vexiau had gone away for the weekend. We were sitting together on a settee talking when I felt I could no longer hide my feelings from her. I was delighted to find that she was as much in love with me as I was with her.

The day before Christmas Phyllis received a very unwelcome Christmas gift—the mumps! It was almost inevitable as Martine, Madame Vexiau's granddaughter from upstairs, had come down with them the week before. As she had a very mild case, Martine spent most of her time downstairs, even though everyone knew Phyllis had not had the mumps. As I had had the mumps as a child, I was only too happy to look after Phyl, bringing her meals, making her comfortable, and keeping her company to help her pass the time. This continued for another ten days after the mumps, as they were followed by a very severe case of conjunctivitis which kept her in bed. All this wonderful companionship and closeness only helped to deepen our love for each other.

In early January we felt we should let our parents know of our feelings for one another, to see what their reaction would be. They were very happy for us, with their only concern being the difference in our ages. During our courtship, they never tried to influence our decision, one way or the other. We both felt if it was the Lord's will for us to marry, the difference in our ages would not be a problem. We had also let the Field Counsel in Africa, my Pastor and the Eston Church Board know of the possibility of us getting married. Their replies were also favorable. There was, however, one problem that caused Phyllis some hesitation. In the past, when she had wondered about marriage, the Lord had given her the Scripture, Isaiah 54:5: —"For your Creator is your husband..." How could she now, go against what she had felt so definitely to be the counsel of the Lord to her? I assured Phyllis that even though I loved her more than anything in this world, if she ever felt that the Lord was asking her to remain single, I would not in any way stand in her way. The Lord's will for our lives was of supreme importance.

Some months previous, the Field Counsel, while revising Field Policy, had passed a resolution to the effect that single missionaries would no longer be accepted—Phyllis being an exception, because of the nature of her ministry. If we didn't marry, I would have to return to Canada and would have to find a wife before I could get to Upper Volta. Well aware of my previous record at romance, the prospects did not look particularly good. However, I had learned to trust the Lord in many different circumstances, so surely I could trust Him to touch some young lady's sympathetic heart who had a call to the mission field. I had also thought at times that should Phyllis and I marry, some people might think that, for my part, it was just a marriage of convenience, so that I could go directly on to Africa.

We decided that until we were sure it was the Lord's will for us to marry, we would have to modify our relationship. Because of spending so much time together as lovers, our French had really suffered. As we were being supported in France to learn the language, we would just have to "knuckle down" and concentrate on language study. It was not easy to change our relationship with us living so close together and seeing each other so often, but we just had to trust the Lord to give us the needed grace and strength. For the next several weeks we did manage to get back to regular classes and study time. I also enrolled in an evening Bible Course sponsored by Child Evangelism International. Not only did it reduce the time we would otherwise be together in the evenings, but it also helped me with the spiritual vocabulary I would need that was not being taught at Alliance.

Sunday afternoons, Phyllis and I had been joining other missionaries who met at the home of a young French couple. There were refreshments during a time of fellowship, followed by a time of singing, testimonies and prayer. After a short meditation from the Word by the man of the house, a delicious meal was served. It was a wonderful break from a week of intense studying. The last Sunday evening in April, on our way home, we walked through the Bois de Boulogne. We stopped on an old, rustic wooden bridge over a stream running into the lake. As we talked, I reached out, putting my hand over hers. In an instant, we were in each other's arms. I asked her if she would marry me, and on one knee I held out the only ring I could afford to offer her—my signet ring. Without hesitation, she said she would. We had both, for the last short while, been feeling the Lord had given the green light for us to marry. She said she had been reading Song of Solomon and been impressed with 8:7, "Many waters cannot quench love, neither can the floods drown it". Since

Bible School days the Lord had brought our lives together in so many different ways, it seemed only right now to make it permanent. We walked home on "Cloud Nine" that evening.

Chapter 14

MY WIFE TO BE

PHYLLIS LAVERNE BURR WAS BORN ON MAY 23, 1916, to Percival and LaVerne (Yeager) Burr, in New Westminster, BC, the first of four children. Phyllis's father was a Real Estate Agent with Pemberton's in Vancouver. He was one of their top salesmen up until the day of his death at 91. Her Mother, LaVerne Yeager, was from Oklahoma. She was teaching public speaking in Boston when Percy, wanting to improve his oratorical skills, enrolled in her class. After a short courtship, they married and moved back to New Westminster. The family owned a cottage in White Rock overlooking the ocean. A steep path led down to the water and a beautiful beach. Much time during her early years was spent here with family and friends. As the ebb and flow of the tides were considerable, the water was always warm and swimming was excellent. Thus, Phyllis became an excellent swimmer. She loved music and became an accomplished pianist and piano accordionist and had an excellent singing voice. Her mother was a wonderful, committed Christian, though her father was not interested in spiritual things. However, he never seemed to mind his wife inviting her Christian friends for meals. He seemed to enjoy one visitor, in particular, William Booth-Clibborn, the grandson of William Booth, the founder of the Salvation Army.

Booth-Clibborn was a gifted children's evangelist and held children's meetings up and down the west coast. When Phyllis was 8 years old, he came to New Westminster for several days of meetings, and Phyllis along with her 7-year-old sister, June, attended. Booth-Clibborn was a great storyteller and could hold the children's attention. The children loved his stories so much they didn't want to leave at noontime; they brought their lunch and stayed all day. It was during these meetings that Phyllis, along with her sister, June, invited Jesus into her life. Her commitment to Jesus Christ at that time had a profound influence on the rest of her life.

After High School, Phyllis wanted to take nurses' training. But Canada was in the throes of the Great Depression and many businesses fell on tough times, including Pemberton's. Her Dad suggested she choose a profession that would allow her to quickly begin making a living. She chose teaching and completed one year at Columbia College before attending Vancouver Normal School from which she graduated with distinction in 1936. She began teaching on Vancouver Island. As there was a demand for English and Music in the larger schools, she attended Summer School in Victoria and received a Music Specialist Certificate. For 9 years she taught on Vancouver Island, in New Westminster, and in Vancouver.

In 1945 she took a leave of absence from teaching to attend Full Gospel Bible Institute in Eston, SK. She so enjoyed her first year that she resigned from public school teaching and planned to return as a student to FGBI. However, before the second year began, she was contacted by the School Board with an offer to join the staff to teach English, Music and Child Evangelism. She'd had her heart set on a second year of studies but accepted the position, hoping she would still have time to attend some classes. She found little time for classes as she was also asked to be music director and, the following year, the choir director.

Phyllis and I were classmates at FGBI in 1945 but the following year she was one of my teachers. We sometimes sang duets together with the accordion, and sometimes she accompanied me on the piano when I was invited to sing. She also played the piano for the FGBI radio broadcast over the Prince Albert station and we were occasionally invited to sing a duet.

During the summer months she was involved in ministry in various churches--children's meetings, filling in for Pastors on holidays, tent evangelism, and for several years, at Veteran Gospel Camp as the camp pianist and in children's ministry. At Veteran Camp, there was always one day of the week set aside for missions, with several missionaries and missionary candidates participating. Greatly influenced by these meetings, it was at Veteran camp that she first felt the Lord calling her to be a missionary. During the visit of the Davies brothers to FGBI, she was invited to Upper Volta as a teacher for the missionaries' kids. That summer, at Veteran Camp, after one of the evening services, she was at the altar praying, considering the Davies' invitation. She confessed later that she told the Lord she was afraid to go to Upper Volta because she was afraid of the wild animals. As she was praying, the Holy Spirit prompted her to sing the chorus of a well-known hymn:

> O hallelujah, yes, 'tis Heav'n,
> 'Tis Heaven to know my sins for-giv'n.

She stopped singing there and said to the Lord: "But Lord, it is not this that is my problem! I know I'm saved". But she felt urged to continue with the rest of the chorus:

> On land or sea, what matters where?
> Where Jesus is, 'tis Heaven there.

Immediately the Holy Spirit flooded her heart with peace and joy as she yielded to the will of the Lord.

Invited back to Veteran Camp again in the summer of 1950, she was asked to take part in a day set apart for Missions. She made the camp aware that the Lord had called her to be a missionary and that she had been invited to the Upper Volta Mission to teach the Mission kids. As Upper Volta was a French Colony at that time, she said it was necessary to spend a year learning the French language, preferably in Paris. At this point, she had no financial support, and was hoping that something might be done for her at Camp. She was very disappointed when, after the last Sunday meeting, nothing had been. People were getting up out of their seats and would soon be leaving camp for home.

A man from the small town of Flaxcombe, a regular attendee at Camp, called out for the people to sit back down for a moment. He said, "There is a young lady who has ministered at the camp for several years, who has been called by the Lord as a missionary to

Upper Volta. She needs to spend a year in language study in France, and she needs support during that time." He said he would like to see enough raised by an offering and pledges to pay for her fare to and from France and to support her monthly while studying in France. That afternoon, when the offering and pledges were tallied up, there was sufficient to do just that. The Lord confirmed to Phyllis that day, that when He calls, He is indeed Jehovah-Jireh, the God who provides.

In the spring of 1950, her application to language school in Paris was accepted at the same time as mine. Later we found that we were both booked at the same time on the same ship headed for France. We met in Quebec City in August 1950 to board the Samaria for England and France. From that time on, our lives were pretty well entwined, so much so that we decided in Paris that it was time to join them for the rest of our lives.

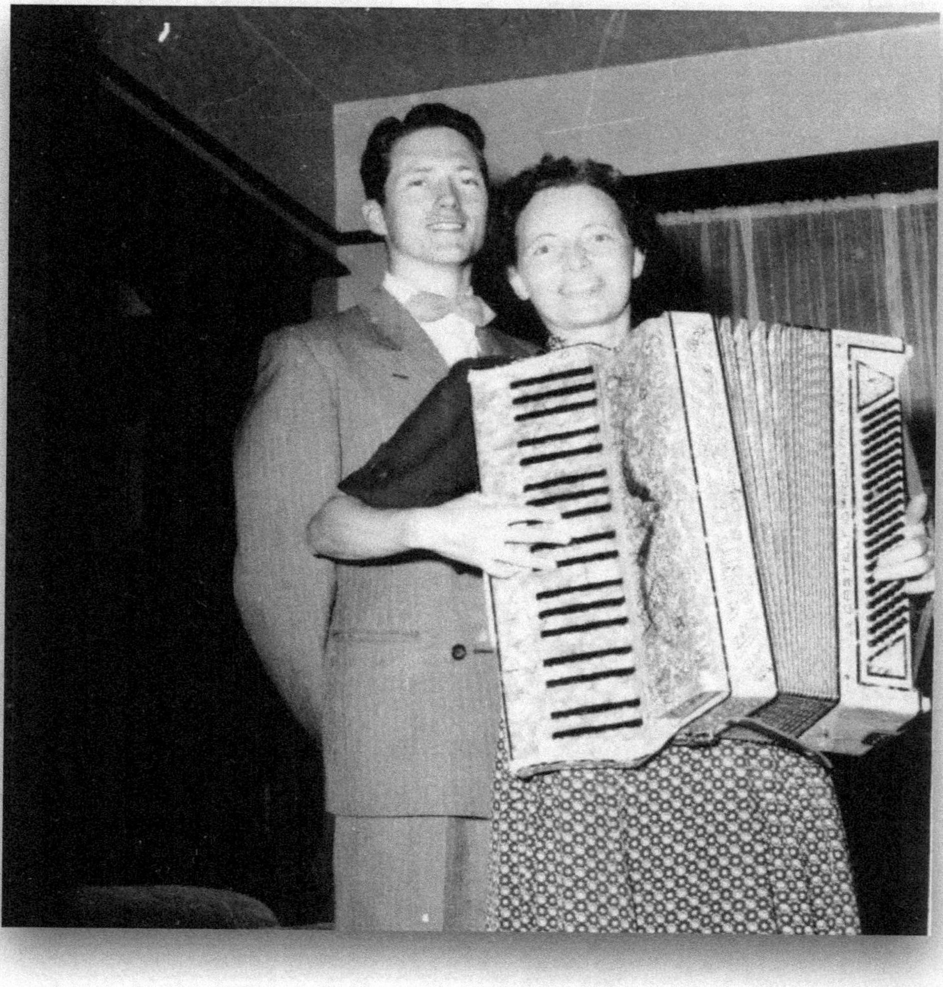

Chapter 15
WEDDING BELLS

WE DECIDED IT WAS TIME TO CONSIDER A DATE FOR our wedding. We were thinking of the first week in May for several reasons. As both our birthdays were in May, we thought it would be good to have our anniversary the same month. We wanted the month of June free to study for an important final exam at the end of the month. Art and Greta Sheppard, friends from FGBI years, were planning a European Evangelistic Crusade in the summer sponsored by Youth for Christ and wanted Phyllis and me to join them. We felt it would be much more appropriate if we were married before travelling with them.

In France only a civil wedding is recognized; a religious ceremony is optional. Our Pastor, being from the UK, informed us that the British Consul was authorized to officiate weddings. As we found that the Canadian Ambassador was unable, we accepted the earliest date at the British Consulate, May 28th, 1951. A young missionary couple, Jim and Ruth Riccitelli, whom we had met at Alliance, and Madame Vexiau, were our witnesses. The Vice-Consul and the Acting British Consul-General performed the "ceremony".

This consisted mainly of signing papers, swearing upon the Bible that all statements were true, and the hesitant announcement by the Consul General, as he threw up his arms, "Well...I guess...I pronounce you husband and wife!" We were certainly glad we were able to have a church service afterward, or I don't think either of us would have felt married with only that little bit of a ceremony.

The church was already beautifully decorated with flowers as the day before had been Mother's Day. Phyllis and I sat in chairs in the centre aisle of the auditorium with Jim and Ruth as our attendants. From the pulpit, Pastor Roberts read and commented on Ephesians 5:22-23, emphasizing verse 22 "Wives submit to your own husbands as to the Lord," and verse 25 "Husbands, love your wives, just as Christ also loved the church..."

He then came down, stood in front of us, had us stand, and using the Anglican Prayer Book went through the ceremony. When he came to the part, "Wives obey your husbands," I couldn't resist the temptation to give Phyllis a gentle nudge. I don't know if anyone in the congregation saw it, but Phyllis did! All we could afford for rings were two plain gold bands which he placed on the Bible before we exchanged them. After pronouncing us "husband and wife," he presented us with a French Bible and spent several minutes emphasizing the importance of the Word in our marriage, and our individual lives. To Phyl and me it was a beautiful service, and the presence of the Lord was very real. Madame Vexiau and her son, Robert, told us they were very impressed, as did others of the congregation.

Madame Vexiau had prepared a delicious wedding dinner for us at her home; Pastor and Mrs. Roberts, Jim and Ruth Riccitelli, Robert, his wife, Simone and their three daughters from upstairs, and, of course, Madame. Simone, an outstanding artist, had arranged so artistically the dining room and table with flower bouquets and blossoms strewn around the three-tiered wedding cake that Ruth had made. We moved to the terrace for dessert and coffee, and to enjoy the sunshine. The day had begun cool and overcast but was now sunny and warm. Phyllis opened the wedding gifts we had received and read the cablegrams from our parents and home churches.

Pastor Roberts drove us to the station from where we took the train to the small village of Dampierre, about an hour's ride from Paris. The countryside was beautiful and the weather sunny and warm. They were the nicest days we had seen, except for our wedding day, as it had been cool and rainy for several weeks. We practically had the Inn to ourselves, as there was only one other guest. The meals were excellent, and we had a wonderful relaxing time. All too soon, it was time to return to Paris, and to our studies, in preparation for the final exam.

Finally, the day arrived for the first test that Phyl would have to pass, for her to be able to advance to the next stage needed for her to teach French in Africa. The first part of the examination was a six-hour written test. Only those who passed the written were able to move on to the oral test. Two days later, we were relieved and pleased, to find our names in the list of those who had passed the written. The oral part was not too difficult, although my brain turned to jelly when I was asked to name five flowers. The only one I could think of was "carnation" which is the same in both English and French, only different pronunciations. The professor kept dropping hints until I finally got the five. A few days later we were so happy to see that we had both passed the final and were now entitled to the "Diplome de Langue" (Language Diploma). We could only give thanks and praise to the Lord for making all this possible.

    I decided not to take more classes for the time being, but to spend more time studying the Bible in French and preparing for the coming months of ministry with the Sheppards. Phyllis registered for the classes leading to the next diploma, "La Langue Superieure," which she would need for teaching in Upper Volta. She began feeling very tired, which we thought was from all the heavy studying in preparation for the exam, but when she also started feeling nauseous we thought it was time for her to have a physical checkup. To say the least, we were incredibly surprised to find that she was pregnant. We hadn't discussed plans for a family, and it was certainly not a very propitious time to start one. There was a French Doctor, Dr. Binet, practicing in Paris at the Hertford British Hospital who was willing to take care of Phyllis during the pregnancy.

    Some weeks later, we were invited along with others to dinner and an evening in the home of an American couple who were also preparing as missionaries. During the evening, Phyllis complained of feeling faint and dizzy and of having cramps. One of the American guests was a Doctor who found Phyllis was on the verge of having a miscarriage. Having a car, he drove us to the British Hospital where Dr. Binet confirmed the diagnosis and had Phyl admitted. After the Doctors had left, the head nurse told me that it was very unlikely that

Phyllis would be able to keep the baby. However she did, and five days later was allowed to come home. The Doctor advised plenty of bed rest and no heavy lifting or exertion.

Later on during the pregnancy, one night Phyl was in a lot of pain and towards morning she began to hemorrhage. I phoned the hospital and was told to bring her in. The head nurse said she thought Phyl was having a miscarriage. The Doctor had told Phyl before that she should rest a lot and stay in bed one week of each month. Phyl hadn't been doing that as she felt so good. She had been told so often that it was unlikely she would be able to keep the baby but every time she did, they told her she would be back. We know it was only the goodness of the Lord that allowed her to carry him thus far, and that he was alive and well.

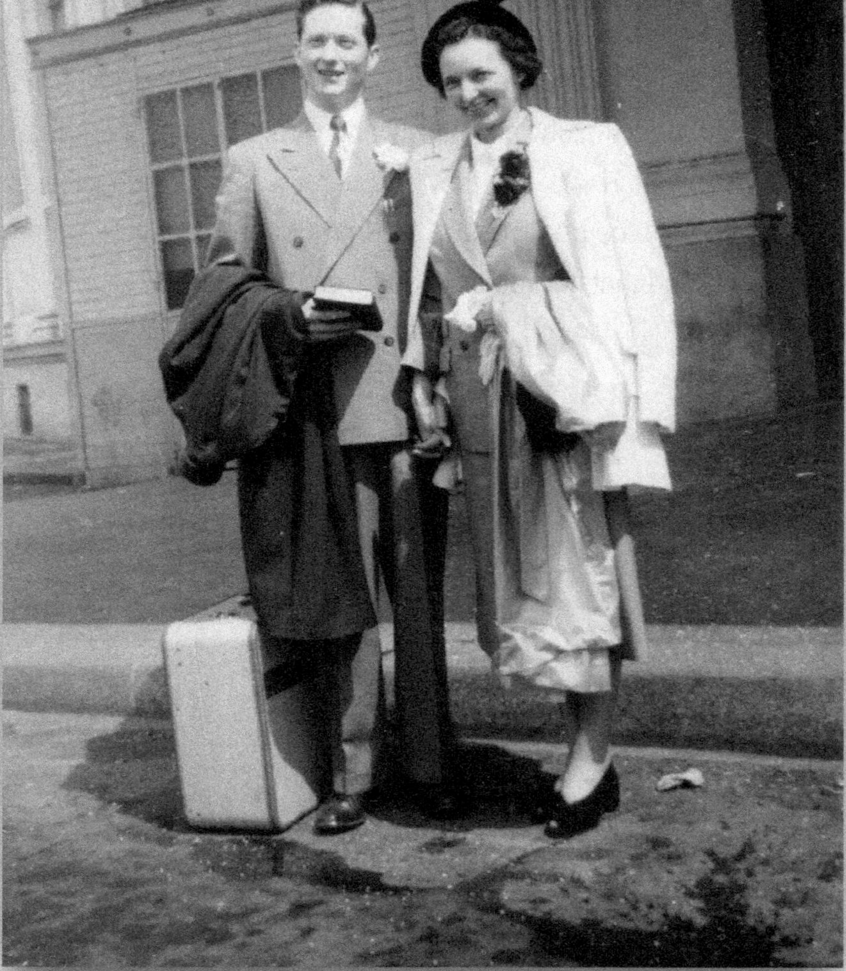

Chapter 16
MINISTRY WITH YOUTH FOR CHRIST

IN JULY, WE WERE DELIGHTED TO RECEIVE A LETTER from Art and Greta Sheppard, inviting Phyl and me to join them in ministry with Youth for Christ over the summer months. This meant we would have to move from Madame Vexiau's and go hunting for a small apartment. However, the doctor did not think it wise for Phyllis to travel because of the pregnancy, and the possibility of a miscarriage. I felt I could not be away and leave her to look after herself in her condition so after much earnest prayer, she insisted that, with the Lord's help, she would be able to take care of herself and that I should go. I promised I would come right back if at any time she felt she could no longer go it alone. Thanks to the Lord, we were able to find an apartment that fit her needs. We also found that within a short walk from our apartment there was a daily street market with an abundance of fresh vegetables and fruits, and across the street were shops selling other necessities. By the time Phyl was ready to leave the hospital, I had moved our few belongings from Madame Vexiau's to our new home.

We both felt we needed to get away for a break. The long hours studying for the Diploma, moving to a new apartment and Phyl's physical ordeal had all taken their toll. We were able to find accommodation at a missionary retreat, Villa Emmanuel, in the Swiss Alps. It was a beautiful place with an abundance of trees, a beautiful view of the mountains and flowers everywhere. The villa had its own gardens, and every meal was deliciously served with fresh vegetables and fruit. There was a Bible study every morning and a devotional service every evening. Daily planned hikes into the countryside were arranged as well as a day-long bus trip. As there was a lot of climbing on the hikes Phyllis remained at the villa and enjoyed relaxing in the sun and breathing in the delightful mountain air. We returned home refreshed both physically and spiritually.

Art phoned to let me know that we were booked for Portugal for two months, that they planned to come to Paris and, together, on September 16, we would be on our way by train. It was a long tearful goodbye with my darling as we waited for a taxi to take us to the Austerlitz Train Station. Our departure time was 10:20 p.m. and an hour before time to leave, the train was already crowded but we were able to find three seats together. As we pulled away from the platform, I was standing at the window looking out over the city thinking of Phyl alone in our apartment. I prayed she would sense the Divine Presence of the Lord as never before and feel safe and protected under His sheltering wings.

By noon the next day, we were at the French border city of Hendaye. It was blistering hot on the platform where we waited for the Spanish connecting train. We went through French customs and, an hour later, the train to Irun, the Spanish border town, arrived, and in a few minutes we were in Spain. There again, we waited on the platform, under a blazing sun, for almost an hour before the Spanish Authorities showed up. With the border formalities over, we were able to get a break from the sun as we were allowed into the station.

We had brought some food from home to eat along the way. We had had an early breakfast on the train, so were famished. At 3:30 in the afternoon, under the shade of a few trees, we ate our lunch. The tomatoes had gotten squashed, but they were still edible and tasted good with bread and boiled eggs. We had fresh pears for dessert.

Even though we had tickets from Paris to Portugal, we had to buy reservations to continue. When we returned from lunch there was already a long line-up at the ticket wicket. All that was available were a few seats in third class. The conductor informed us we would have to sit in one of the last two cars as at 4:00 a.m. the cars would be dropped at Medina, and later, picked up by a train headed for the Portuguese border. As the last two cars were already crowded, we moved into the second class car and found an empty compartment. We were soon joined by a man, two Australian girls, and later by two nuns. The nuns tried speaking with us and I found I could understand a little Portuguese. I indicated to them we were going to Medina and then on to Portugal, and they both said, "No! No!" I couldn't understand what they were trying to tell us, or the conductor who came by later, but we knew what we had to do, so we played dumb. The conductor, who was getting more and more agitated, finally threw his arms up in the air and with an "I-yi-yi-yi-yi" walked away. One of the Nuns found a piece of paper and on it wrote 4:00 a.m. They were trying to tell us we were in the wrong car and would have to move. When I assured them we knew we would have to move but that now all the seats were full, they said they were afraid we might sleep and not wake in time to catch our train

About 8:30 that evening, we rationed out what was left of our meager lunch so that we would each have one egg, one piece of tomato, one piece of bread, and a banana for breakfast. We then settled down to try and get a little sleep, but it was short-lived. At the next stop, a priest and two other men boarded the train, shoved their baggage into our compartment, and tried to claim our seats. The priest could speak French and told me we would have to move as we were in reserved seats. He became angry when I told him there was nothing to indicate the seats were reserved. When the conductor came by, the priest ordered him to make us move to third class. When the conductor refused, he became even angrier and crowded in between the young lady and the wall, thereby squashing everybody. One of the men with him did likewise on the other side so that we were 10 people in the compartment rather than the usual eight. I spent the rest of the night trying to sleep with one eye open so as not to miss our 4:00 a.m. move.

When the train started to slow down, we grabbed our bags and as soon as it stopped, we made a mad dash down the platform for the rear of the train. We boarded the train and found three seats, but the other five seats were occupied by soldiers, and the compartment reeked to high heaven. A porter showed us to another considerably better compartment. I tried to settle down to a little sleep but met with no success. We weren't long at Medina and at sunrise we were picked up and on our way to Portugal.

The sunrise was extraordinarily beautiful, but what a country it revealed—poor, barren, red soil with a few stunted trees. As it was harvest time in Spain, we passed what looked like whole communities working together in the fields. Oxen were being driven over the piles of straw, trampling out the grain. Other piles of grain were being thrown in the air for the wind to blow away the chaff. How primitive it looked! Pigs were running everywhere, in and out of the hovels, which looked like the people's homes. Each village, however, was dominated by a very imposing cathedral, in strange contrast to where the people were living.

At about 8:00 a.m. we finished our meager breakfast, holding onto an orange each for later as we had no water. About 11:30 a.m. we arrived at the Portuguese border, and again, sat for an hour or more while going through Customs. At Formoso, where we were to change trains, I was passing our baggage out the window to Art on the platform when a young lady approached him. Violeta Lopes, an American missionary working in Portugal, her mother, and a Portuguese pastor, Brother Oliviera were there to meet us. Being met at the border was an answer to prayer. They were surprised at seeing three of us, as they had been expecting only one.

Since the vehicle was much too small to take us all, we would have to continue by train. The Pastor helped us through customs and immigration, then took us to a hotel where he ordered a meal for us. How great it was to be able to wash in a relatively clean washroom, after the filthy, rank washrooms on the train. We ate heartily as it was nearly 3:00 p.m. and we'd had nothing since early morning. The Pastor then bought our tickets through to Leiria and wrote out instructions for us to follow. We were grateful that we had only one change to make. As all the compartments in second class were full, we moved into first class, but when the conductor came by, he made us move back. In one compartment there were three empty seats, but two of them were reserved. We put up our baggage and Greta took the available seat. Art and I sat in the reserved seats, and, thankfully, no one ever did come to claim them. By mid-afternoon we were on our way again but were much more at ease knowing our route was all worked out and that missionaries would be at the other end to meet us. The countryside was interesting—mountainous, with little farms like a patchwork quilt up the sides. You would wonder how they could scratch out a living in such rocky soil.

Exhausted, we slept for about an hour, and woke up hot, sticky and covered with white dust. We tried freshening up in the filthy washroom but felt no better for our efforts. About 6:30, the train stopped at a small station where, fortunately, there was a lady selling pork in a bun and bottled water. A couple of hours later, we arrived at the place to change trains. Two employees there hustled us off the train and hurried us to our connecting train on the other side of the station. We were delighted to find a modern looking car; a bus on rails. When we presented our second class tickets we were told there was no second class and would have to go to third class. A Portuguese gentleman, who spoke English, told us to sit in first class and pay the difference when the conductor came by. However, when he did, we were grateful to Father that he accepted our tickets and we had no extra to pay.

After a fast two-hour ride, we arrived at Leiria and were met by a short, stocky man, another Mr. Oliviera, and his wife. Without even a greeting or a handshake, they grabbed our bags and said, "Let's go!" We piled into a beautiful American Buick with a chauffeur and were whisked off towards the town. I wondered what kind of luxury these pastors were living in, but later, learned the Buick was a taxi.

He was very pleased when Art told him we would be available for two months of ministry, as that would mean we would be able to stay for more than just one service in each location. We were taken to a Hotel, shown to our rooms, and after a quick wash, went to the dining room. At 11 o'clock that night we had our second Portuguese meal. I could scarcely stay awake waiting my turn to hit the shower. When I did, I feared the accumulated dust and dirt of the past couple of days and nights might plug the drain! How wonderful the hot water felt, but it was even more wonderful to feel the nice clean, cool sheets. I couldn't feel them for long for even as I was thanking the Lord for a clean, soft bed, I dropped off into a deep sleep. We were so grateful to the Lord that we would be free of trains for a while.

Chapter 17

Ministry in Portugal

IN THE MORNING, FROM MY HOTEL WINDOW, I HAD A good view of the city. In front was a river lined with trees. All the houses were white or yellow with red tile roofs. Situated on a high hill were the ruins of a castle looking impressive against the skyline, and on another hill, a sight we would get used to seeing—a huge catholic church dominating the city. I was amazed at the extremes in the traffic—American cars, small donkey and ox carts, and bare-footed women carrying water jugs, loaded baskets, and other things on their heads. For the first two weeks we were with the Baptist Mission and held meetings in two churches. The first night the service was to be in a neighboring town, but we were beginning to wonder if there was going to be a service, as at 9:00 pm no one had come to take us to the church. Eventually, we were picked up, and when we arrived at the church were surprised to find few people. We met the pastor who invited us to a back room to discuss the service and have prayer. When we went out to the platform later there were well over 300 people gathered! We found this to be the same throughout the country. Most of the rural people work until dark then walk to church, often several kilometers and many of them without having eaten supper. Businesses in the cities closed during the heat of the afternoon and then remained open until late in the evening.

What a rousing welcome we received as we were introduced in our first service. We brought greetings from Canada and gave a brief testimony. Art preached on Isaiah 1:18 and thus ended our first service in Portugal. Afterward, we shook hands with nearly all 300 at the meeting! It was after midnight by the time we were driven to our Hotel. The bed that felt so wonderful the night before didn't feel so good that night as I tried to get comfortable. The mattress was full of humps and hollows, but all in the wrong places. If it had just hollowed where I humped, we would have gotten along just fine.

During the two weeks we were with the Baptist Mission, there were 53 decisions for Christ: 25 adults and 28 children. Their names were recorded so each one could be followed up and integrated into the church. Violeta Lopes was to be our chauffeur and interpreter for the rest of our time. For our second week we were put up in an old hotel that was not only dirty but very noisy until the wee hours of the morning. Because of the unsanitary conditions and because most meals in Portugal contain whole fish floating in olive oil (awfully hard on most foreigners' digestive systems), we decided to get our own meals. For the rest of our time in Portugal, the ladies did the cooking and Art and I did the cleaning up.

As the church had only been started five months earlier by a student from the Baptist Bible School, the majority of the Christians were comprised of new converts who'd had little Bible teaching. The young Pastor was delighted that the crowds for the services were increasing night after night and by the end of the second week, there had been 50 decisions for Christ. Children's meetings accounted for 28 accepting the Lord while 22 adults took the step of faith. Again, the names of each new convert was recorded so they could be contacted and followed up by the church.

Monday was a day off so we drove back to Vi's home in Leiria to prepare for our move to a new area where we would be working with another Mission. At noon we packed a lunch and drove to the nearby beach for some relaxation. The water was wonderfully warm with white-capped breakers, as the tide was coming in. We swam off and on and relaxed in the sun while reading or writing letters. When it was time to retire that night, we realized we had not been wise to spend so much time in the sun without any protection. Trying to sleep for the next several days proved unpleasant.

We were to spend the first week of September with the Brethren Mission under the leadership of Frank Smith. He and his wife were from the UK and had been ministering in central Portugal for many years. They'd been introduced to Pentecost and had both been baptized in the Holy Spirit. They were not being financially supported by any mission society but living entirely by faith. Their ministry during the past several years had been like a page out of the Book of Acts. They had established and were overseeing 14 local churches, each having its own Pastor. Years later, Frank Smith was invited to Canada to visit the ECP churches and speak at the Annual General Conference which was being held in Eston that year.

The meetings were well attended, often as many people were gathered outside the church as inside. The results during the two weeks were very satisfying as people were wonderfully restored to fellowship with the Lord, some beautifully healed, others baptized in the Holy Spirit, and others being set free from demon oppression. At least 35 adults and 23 children came to the Lord for salvation. The following week we were with the Methodist Mission in a city of about 10,000 where many of the congregation were from well-to-do families. Unlike previous meetings, there was no life to the singing or response to the Holy Spirit, despite all our efforts. All in all, it was a disappointing week. The only bright spot was that at least 15 children had invited Jesus into their lives.

Our next stop was with the Baptist Mission for a week. There was good attention to the Word as Art preached, and during the week about 80 people were dealt with for salvation, as well as a good number of young ones in the children's meetings. During the mornings, the ladies would have meetings for the children while Art and I would hand out tracts, specially to ladies gathered at the streams doing their laundry. We sold Bibles, hymnbooks, and other books in Portuguese for a very nominal price. We were told the people would respect and care for what they bought themselves more than for what was handed out to them, something that I later found to be true in Africa as well.

For our last week of services, we were back with Frank Smith. It felt like being back home as we were free to pray for the sick and for people to be baptized in the Spirit. Four of the villages, where Frank had just started meetings, only had a few Believers. The Pastor supervising the churches had been saved as a young lad and had earned a New Testament at Sunday School. As he had been caught reading it and had been beaten several times by his parents, he used to take it to read while watching the sheep. When his Uncle, a catholic priest, discovered his Bible, he too, beat him, tore it up, and threatened him. With tears in his eyes, the little lad replied, "You can tear my Bible up, but you can't tear Jesus out of my heart."

Many young people came out of curiosity and stayed outside, laughing and scoffing. Because of the strong Catholic influence, the Christians had suffered much persecution but had remained steadfast in their faith. By the end of the week, nine people had responded to the altar calls for salvation.

We were to spend our last few days in Portugal with two Pentecostal churches in Lisbon, the Capital City. On Monday, October 1st, we said goodbye to the Smiths and retraced our steps to say goodbye to the others with whom we had worked. We arrived in Lisbon in the late afternoon, and soon found the home of the Stahlberg's, from Sweden and the Bowkers, from the UK. About 10:00 pm, as the folks were going out to a meeting, they left supper for us. We were thankful for an evening off, and after writing another letter to Phyl and walking to a mailbox five minutes away to post it, I was ready for bed.

The next day, it was time to buy my ticket back to Paris. It seemed to take forever at American Express with all the paperwork involved, but two hours later, I had my fare paid. All I had to do was go back the next day to pick up the ticket, or so I thought. The following day I was informed that the Cheque I had issued the day before was not valid. After another lengthy session and much discussion, the problem was solved. Thanks to the Lord's intervention, I finally had my return ticket in my hand.

Our first meeting in Lisbon was in a beautiful hall, seating about 200, with a Portuguese pastor in charge. One lady came forward for salvation at the altar call. Afterward, there was time to pray for the sick, and thirty or more responded. We didn't get home until after 2:00 am and found lunch on the table at the Bowkers.

Our second meeting was held in a new chapel, seating around 1,000. When we arrived, much to our surprise, there was an estimated crowd of 700. One lady responded as Art gave the altar call, and as Brother Stahlberg took over to close the service, two more came forward. After the service, another young lady, deeply under conviction, asked for prayer and surrendered her life to Jesus. It was her first time, ever, in a Gospel service. Before we left the church, two members of the church asked for prayer for healing.

As a team, we felt God had vindicated and confirmed His Word in our meetings. We were told there were over 200 conversions, including children, with several believers restored to fellowship as well as many baptized in the Holy Spirit and wonderfully healed. The names were taken of all the converts to be followed up by their local church. We were able to present New Testaments to every convert, including children and hundreds of tracts were distributed.

Several Evangelistic teams visited Portugal each year and all followed the same circuit as we had. How we wished we could have gone into an area that had never had a Gospel witness. The problem was that there would be no one to follow up as there were not enough workers. There were only 50 workers altogether for Portugal's 8 million people.

Art Sheppard and Stan in Portugal

Portugal, 1951

Chapter 12
MINISTRY IN PARIS & IRELAND

THE FOLLOWING MORNING, I PACKED MY SUITCASES, ready for the train that would start me on my way back to Paris and my wife. I made the rounds to say goodbye to our Missionary hosts, the Portuguese Pastors and Violeta Lopes, who'd become such an important member of our team. I would be meeting up later with Art and Greta who were going to find out where our next assignment with Youth for Christ would be. The train seemed to run at a snail's pace as the morning stretched into afternoon. Finally, after it seemed as though the sun would never set, the lights of Paris appeared in the distance.

Would the love of my life be waiting on the platform to welcome me home? I hardly thought so, as just a week ago she had moved into a new apartment. Some time before, we had made arrangements with another missionary couple so that when they left for the mission field, we would take their suite. They had left for the field much sooner than they had expected, and it had fallen on Phyl in her condition to pack up all our things, get a dray to haul them to the new place, to unpack and get the place to look like a home.

I held my breath as I exited the platform, searching the crowd, and yelled: "Praise the Lord!" as I spotted her. Phyl had become friends with an American classmate and she and her husband had offered to drive her to meet the train. I rushed over to take her in my arms, as much of her as I could as she was quite a size by now! We were soon making up for all the hugs and kisses we had missed over the past months.

We gave thanks to the Lord for watching over Phyl and prayed for wisdom to know what to do about continuing on with the Youth for Christ team. The team would be arriving soon in Paris for meetings in Brother Roberts' church before going on to Ireland. We went to see the Doctor who gave us his approval, but said I should be prepared to come back home as quickly as possible, should she need me.

The meetings ran from October 18 to the 24th. Brother Roberts wanted me to interpret for the meetings; I felt inadequate but knew I could fall back on him if I couldn't handle it. Phyllis wanted to have a part in the meetings and felt she could play the piano, which she did for most of the services. She had to spend the last weekend in bed though, as it was that time of the month when she needed to do nothing but rest. The folks were billeted out to members of the congregation, where they also got their breakfast. They were with us for several meals, however, and Phyl found it quite a chore to prepare special meals for them in her condition.

Brother Roberts was very pleased with how the meetings were going. They were certainly wonderfully blessed of the Lord with many being saved, especially among the women, many healed and others delivered from demon oppression. Towards the end of the week, so many were coming up for prayer that we had to form two prayer lines; one for Art and another for me. It seemed so many of the women in the church were delving into spiritism. Of those who came for prayer, most wanted to be set free from Satan's bondage. One woman had been put under a satanic spell of blindness six years ago as the result of her interest in spiritism, and her turning against it. The Doctors could find nothing wrong with her eyes; the spell had been put on her by another woman spiritist. But, after she was prayed for, she said she felt life coming into her eyes for the first time in all those years. Praise the Lord! There were many other testimonies of healings as well.

    I remained at home for a few days while Art and Greta went on to Ireland as I wanted to be alone with Phyl. The past week had been quite strenuous for her and I wanted to be sure everything was all right. I hated to leave her alone, but as we agreed, the faithful saints at Eston and from Veteran Camp were not supporting us to have a baby, but either to be actively engaged in the Lord's work, or preparing for it. She felt she would be fine, and I promised I would come back as quickly as possible if she needed me.

    A cable from Art asked me to join them in Ireland, as everything was now set for a month of meetings. Following that, in December, we would be in Wales and England. On my way to Ireland, I stopped in England to make arrangements to buy some equipment for Africa, and then took the train and Irish Sea ferry to Belfast. A short bus ride took me to the town where our meetings were to be held. The YFC director welcomed me to his home, where a most delicious roast beef supper with an abundance of fresh vegetables was waiting.

Northern Ireland, during the war years, was asked to contribute to the war effort by providing food for the troops. Every available space, including most golf courses, had been plowed up and turned into crops. An abundance of butter and eggs were sent to the troops along with meat, bacon and vegetables of all kinds. The farmers, of course, had access to all this produce that was available only to others in small amounts with ration cards.

I realized this after a visit to my stepfather's relatives outside of Belfast. His brother worked in a linen factory and I met him when he came home for his noon meal. I wondered why his wife didn't join us, and instead served us one pork chop each with a small spoonful of vegetables. It wasn't until I was back on the bus that it came to me, I had probably eaten his wife's ration of meat for the entire week. I felt so badly, because here I was going back to the farm where everything was abundantly available.

I was surprised to see that Art had invited Andy Stann, a former Bible School student and a western gospel singer to join us for the rest of the tour. Of course, he had his guitar, and he and I sang many duets together and trios when Greta joined us. We began our meetings in a Presbyterian church with around 50 people. The second night there was double that and the third night there was standing room only. It was decided we would move to the town hall which sat around 500 people. By moving into the hall, it meant we could also switch to a more YFC mode and have much more freedom.

To add a little fun, I decided one evening to have a competition. I showed my naivety by proposing that Andy Stann lead the ladies under 40 and I the ladies over 40, in singing, "The Lion of Judah will break every fetter…" As we were finishing another chorus, the YFC director whispered to me that I should suggest another age, as a lot of women are a little touchy about their age, especially around the age of 40. I suggested 60, which he thought was better. Both sides entered into the song with gusto and sang it over and over again. (The song became a sort of theme song for the rest of the meetings!) I thought this would be a good time to have Art bring the message, which that night resulted in some young people accepting Christ into their lives. The response to the Gospel during the weeks, especially by the young people, was most gratifying.

We were invited by a Polish princess who was married to a British scientist, to visit a castle in South Ireland. After tea, we met with the scientist in his office while waiting for supper to be served. There was a long table in the middle of the room, a large easy chair in one corner, and books from floor to ceiling on three walls. He seemed to know where to find a book, or books, dealing with any subject we were discussing at the table. He would ask one of us to get a certain book which he opened at a page that dealt with the subject we were talking about. When we were discussing how to make the Word of God more effective, he had us get a book that he opened and read: "…raise the temperature…" He said He had to go, but asked us to meditate on that. He believed his brother's spirit haunted the castle garden, and at sundown they always met. A verse that came to me about raising the temperature was 1 Peter

1:12 where the prophets: "...preached the Gospel to you by the Holy Spirit sent from heaven..."

After a delicious supper, we set out to explore the castle. The lower floor was full of medieval armor and the second floor, by old agriculture machinery. We found a forge and were surprised to find the old blower still worked and gave off a very eerie, spooky "oooOOOooo." There was a young Church of England missionary staying in one of the rooms. We thought we would like to meet him and have some fun at the same time. I threw a sheet over my head and Art and Andy carried the blower. We knocked on the door and when he appeared, Art and Andy started the blower and I began to dance what I thought was a good spooky, ghostly dance. He stood for a moment, then asked: "Can I do something for you gentlemen?" We were instantly deflated. I was glad I was covered in a sheet and I'm sure Art and Andy wished they were as well. We slunk away as he went inside and shut the door.

After lunch the next day, we went out in a street in Dublin, set up our gear, and started to sing some choruses. As Art began to preach, a man came barging out of the crowd yelling: "Are you Catholic? Are you Catholic?" When Art tried to explain that we were there to talk about Jesus, the man, apparently very drunk, made a rush at Art, fists flailing, knocking him to his knees. Men from the crowd held the man while we loaded all our gear in the vehicle. I heard one lady say to another that she wished the Christians from the North would stay in the North and let us reach our own people.

I was asked to speak to the men in one of the nearby shipyards on a Friday afternoon. There was one of the workers, a Christian, who wanted to share the gospel, but who was too shy. He wouldn't even look at you when talking to you. He would look down, stutter, and talk almost in a whisper. He bought all the loudspeaker equipment, which he would set up when he found someone to present the Gospel. Later that evening I heard there had been a man in the meeting who was going through a hard time, who had finally yielded to the Holy Spirit and had put his confidence in Christ.

The last Saturday night, YFC night, the hall was filled to capacity. Many of the townspeople, young and old, brought their instruments so the music was fantastic. Again there were those of all ages who responded to the altar call. The YFC director said he was pleased with the results of the meetings and invited us back in the future.

We had to catch a late flight to Cardiff, Wales, where we were to minister the next day. There was no one at the airport to meet us, and sometime after Art had put through a phone call, two vehicles showed up, one for Art and Greta and one for Andy and me. As their car was leaving, Art told us he would not be preaching Sunday morning and that we would have to decide who would take the morning service.

When we got to our room, there was a letter from Phyl waiting for me. I tore it open and cried out to the Lord: "Oh God! Undertake for Phyl!" She had written asking me to come home as quickly as possible, as there had been a problem with the baby. Andy and I committed Phyl and the baby to the Lord and prayed for a safe trip home for me. There was no plane from Cardiff, so I had to take the train to London. As I would have to wait until later to get a plane to Paris—I called a man, T. Austin-Sparks, whose writings I had become acquainted with through Frank Smith in Portugal. He was having a Bible study with several young people and invited me to join. I knew then he was a man of the Word and I wanted some of his books. I ended up with several as well as a subscription to his magazine; *A Witness And A Testimony*.

Sunday afternoon I caught the plane to Paris, got a taxi, and headed for home, not knowing what to expect. The Doctor and nurses had said many times, they didn't like the chances of the baby surviving. When she started having pains, Phyl called the Doctor, thinking she was having a miscarriage. He had admitted her to the hospital but discharged her as soon as I arrived home. He said things had settled down, but said she should not be left alone anymore.

Chapter 19

Big Surprise comes in small package

It was hard to realize that Christmas was only a month away. As the day approached, I told Phyl I would like to get the Christmas dinner if she'd let me, and she agreed. No turkeys were showing in the shops yet, mostly geese, but I hoped that closer to Christmas turkeys would appear. I mentioned none of this to Phyl as I wanted it to be a surprise. In the meantime, there was much that had to be done, mainly writing letters and Christmas cards and catching up with correspondence that had been set aside. Altogether we thought we owed 40 or more, but soon had sent out over 90, with more to go.

Christmas Eve came and we were enjoying a lovely evening together in our little apartment and couldn't help but praise the Lord for all His bountiful goodness to us. Phyl had our little home looking so cozy and festive. We had a lovely wood fire in the fireplace, the radio playing Christmas music, a small, decorated Christmas tree with gifts beneath it, flowers, tangerines and an assortment of nuts on the table. Outside a strong wind was blowing, making it seem all the cozier within. How we thanked the Lord for all the material comforts He allowed us to enjoy, but above all, we praised Him for Christ, His unspeakable gift, whom He sent into the world to die, that all who believe in Him might have everlasting life.

Neither turkeys nor chickens ever did appear in the meat shops, just geese and ducks. Christmas morning, I was able to get a good-sized chicken through our concierge whose husband was a farmer. As we had no oven, it had to be cooked in the pressure cooker. The cost of the chicken was almost as much as what I had budgeted for all the other ingredients! I had found a shop where I could get most of what I needed for a truly Canadian feast—creamed corn, sweet potatoes, turnips, turkey dressing and plum pudding with sauce. We ate at about 3:00, then later in the evening had chicken sandwiches and pumpkin pie with whipped cream.

We read more of the Christmas story and had a time of devotions and prayer before we turned to the gifts from families which were waiting for us under the tree. The rest of the evening we continued relaxing and loving each other on the divan that was pulled in front of the fireplace, enjoying tangerines and nibbling nuts.

For New Year's Eve, we again lit the fireplace. Firewood was expensive in Paris, but this would very likely be the last time we would be able to use it. We sat on the divan reading promises from the Word, watching the hands of the clock slowly crawling towards the midnight hour. We had the radio on and heard the crackle of the fireworks as the New Year arrived at different areas of the world. Finally, the midnight hour arrived in Paris. We hugged and prayed and pledged our love for each other and the Lord, even as we had on our wedding day several months earlier.

We now had to turn our attention to what we were supposed to be doing in Paris. We both enrolled for language study again. In her condition, once a week was all that Phyl was able to take at Alliance, but we were able to have an instructor come twice a week to the suite. However, all our plans were short-lived. At 6:00 pm, January 5th, 1952, Phyllis gave birth to a tiny baby boy, Michael Robert Burr King!

We were certainly not expecting this and the suddenness with which he came left us dumbfounded, to say the least, and we had to keep pinching ourselves to make sure that it was real and not just a dream. The night prior, we had not the faintest idea that we would be the parents of a live baby boy today.

We were unprepared for this. We seemed to be living in a daze. Here, suddenly out of the blue and with no warning, we found we had a little life in our care. The birth of a baby was generally left in the hands of the midwives, but because of her history, there were two Doctors as well when Michael came. Normally ten days is when the mothers can go home, but the Doctors wanted Phyl to stay a few extra days, until they thought she was strong enough to look after herself and the baby.

This meant I was going to have to go on a shopping spree to get the things Phyl would need as soon as she and the baby arrived home. I had to start washing baby diapers from the hospital until I found a diaper service. I had to buy a bath, a change table, a heater for the bathroom, a bassinet, and a small washing machine as well as other things like sheets, nighties, and towels. Phyl was able to nurse the baby but didn't always have sufficient milk, so a supplement was required. I told Phyl that when she got home and was able to look after Michael, I would look after all the other things.

After about a month, Phyl said she felt able to handle everything, so I started classes each morning again at the school. Later on, we changed roles and Phyl started classes. It was more important for her to take classes as in January she wanted to write the exams for the Diplome de Langue Superior (Superior Language Diploma) that she would need to teach French in Africa. However, a letter from the Field Council said it seemed less and less likely that the Upper Volta Government was going to approve a school for the Mission. Phyl was encouraged to get the Superior Diploma nevertheless.

I had been accused of having my own agenda and that I had gone to France against the wishes of the Field Council and that I was trying to dictate how much French I would need and when I would be going on to the field. None of this was true, of course. Three founding missionary families were drawing up a Field Policy. I had talked with one of them while he and his wife were still at home in Canada on furlough. He had his wife, who was French, write a letter of application to a language school in Paris. On the ship as they were on their way back to Upper Volta, he wrote me a letter urging me to go to France and after sufficient French, carry on to the field. He said even if I was not able to get the equipment I needed, just come with a camp cot and they would find a place for me. The third member of the Field Council had just arrived home in Canada on furlough and when he saw the letter, he gave his approval to my going to France. With the approval of two of the three founding families, I had set sail for language school.

Besides not accepting single missionaries, the Field Policy would require that they take some sort of training, decided by the Council. In my case, it was to take a course in mechanics. There was also a decision that any equipment purchased while at home and brought to the field would belong to the missionary. But, if equipment arrived after the missionary was back on the field, the equipment would belong to the field. Phyllis had wanted an accordion on the field but hadn't wanted to carry it all along; she wanted it shipped to the field after we had arrived. Now, she was obliged to purchase it before we got to the field.

The Evangelistic Tabernacle in Vancouver had decided to make the Upper Volta Mission its missionary project; the church Board was drawing up a Missions Policy. Any church wanting to send missionaries would have to apply to the Tabernacle. The candidate had to have all his finances in place—fare to and from the field, monthly support for the four years on the field, station allowances and workmen's wages—all available to the Tabernacle, before they could go to the field.

The churches on the prairies found those requirements impossible to meet. Their missionary candidates were responsible during their furloughs to raise their own funds--by pledges, by missionary meetings, by donations--for the four years they would be on the field. So, it was back to the Tab board for revision. As all the discussions were done by mail, it was taking forever for the interested parties to come up with something all could agree on.

The Eston church board let us know that if we wished to apply to another mission field, they would support us. If we preferred, they wondered if I would be able to minister in France or Europe until some satisfactory Mission Policy was acceptable to all the concerned parties. As Brother Roberts had talked with me about helping with the youth of the church, and with Phyllis about working with the children, we decided to remain in Paris until things were resolved. Phyllis went back to French classes, as she still wanted to try for the Diploma, even though she wasn't able to take as many classes as she needed.

Finally, the Eston Church Board decided, for various reasons, it would be best if we came home on furlough. If we were to stay in France then go directly to the field, it would mean we wouldn't get a furlough for seven years. The Board was concerned that would be far too much for Phyl, especially since she was pregnant again by this time, and would soon have two babies to care for.

The Board did not see how they could raise the funds required by the Tab policy without us being there to do deputational meetings. Some of the pledges for Phyl's support received at Veteran camp had fallen off, but the Camp Board of Directors was trying to keep the pledges up. All the pledges taken for Phyl's support would run out in July. Phyl wanted to try the exams for the Diploma the end of the month, even though she knew there wasn't much chance of her passing. Many try for it, but very few of them ever pass on the first attempt. Nevertheless, she wanted to try.

Easter Sunday, 1952

Stan feeding Michael his bottle at 4 weeks old

Chapter 20

Return to Canada

IT WAS DECISION TIME AGAIN. DID WE GO TO ESTON and Phyl have the baby there? We would get Doctor and hospital coverage for about $15.00 a year. Or would we go through to New Westminster? Phyl's mother had not been well and was living with her other daughter, June. Phyl said she would not be capable of looking after the Westminster house in her condition and then with two babies to care for as well. We should have known that we need not worry about such things, as the Lord had His plan. The Church secretary had booked our passage on Air France across the Atlantic to Montreal. Our train ticket was for a roomette from Montreal to Saskatoon, and after a few days, from Saskatoon to New Westminster. Phyl's Mom said she was feeling much better, would be moving back home, and be there to help her daughter and her two grandkids.

We were booked to fly on February 16th, 1953. We had to pack up and ship to Canada the few things we did own and would want in Canada and try to sell the other things. It was not easy to say goodbye to so many people we had gotten to know over the almost three years that Paris was our home. We didn't know the Air France flight would make a stop-over in Iceland. While I stayed on the plane with Michael, Phyl went into the restaurant for some snacks. Then she came back to the plane to watch Michael, who was sound asleep lying across our two seats. We didn't know until later that we were being watched by security as there were drugs available, but we were cleared when I came back to the plane. We could see very little of the country, but it certainly wasn't cold.

We had to wake Michael as there was nowhere else to sit. He lay across our laps which meant little or no sleep for us. The hostess suggested putting Michael in a hammock suspended from the luggage bin over the top of the seats. Poor Michael, when he tried to roll onto his side, rolled right out of the hammock and landed on our knees. By the time we arrived in Montreal, we were all exhausted. I had written from France to a lady, Mrs. Ferry, whose son had attended the Health Institute the same year as myself. We needed to boil up a baby bottle and make formula for our train trip. As she had invited us to come, we took a taxi direct to her place. She said she would like to take us out for dinner in the evening, and as she had a night job, she said she would call for us at 5:00 pm.

We went to our hotel and all fell sound asleep. At 5:00 pm she phoned and said she was down in the lobby. The others were still sleeping, and it wasn't long before I was sound asleep again. Mrs. Ferry phoned again at 6:00 pm and said she had booked off her job, and as soon as we got dressed, we would go. She took us to a luxury hotel which was full of diners. We had had to awaken Michael, and still sleepy, he started to cry. We tried holding him, but he kept on crying. I finally had to take him out as he was causing quite a disturbance. When Phyllis had eaten, she took Michael so I could have my supper. We told Mrs. Ferry we were so sorry to have spoiled her evening and thanked her so much for her efforts to try and give us a pleasant time.

We went back to our hotel; soon sound asleep again. We slept until morning and after a quick breakfast, had to pack up and get to the train station. The church secretary had reserved us a roomette with two bunks There was a restaurant car with very good meals. At bedtime, I slept with Michael, or rather tried to sleep, but not much chance as he kept rolling from side to side and kicking all night long.

The night of the 18th, we arrived in Swift Current. Dad and a neighbor, Johnnie James, were waiting for us. After a three and a half-hour drive, we arrived home. There was almost standing room only, as Church members, the kids from my Sunday school class a few years previous, my Uncle Alvin (with whom I had worked as a teenager), Annie, his wife, and of course, my Mom and Dad were there to greet us. Mom rarely got excited, but she certainly was that night as she saw her grandson for the first time. Michael had been used to older people, and he took to Grandma right away. Reluctantly, she allowed others to hold him and he was passed from one to the other. She had prepared a lunch for us as she thought we might be hungry. It was so good, especially as it had been quite some time ago since we had eaten supper on the train. Michael soon got tired, so it was time for bed. Phyl and I were also ready. We were to stay in my old room with a double bed and a crib. We were weary and it wasn't long before we were all asleep.

On Sunday, I was asked to share with the congregation and also the Sunday school. I spoke again on Wednesday, Monday morning at the men's prayer meeting, and Friday at the church prayer meeting. All in all, it was a busy ten days, until it was time to leave to catch the train for New Westminster. After a tearful goodbye, we were on our way to Swift Current. My Dad and Johnnie James drove us to the station.

Soon the train arrived and we found that a roomette had been reserved for us. There was a diner, again with great meals, and an observation car on the second level. We spent a lot of time sitting up there as we travelled through the mountains. What a beautiful sight it is, the handiwork of our Creator. When the train stopped, we walked up and down the platform, observing the mountains and breathing in the clean, fresh smell of the pine trees.

My family knew Phyllis very well from her years at the Bible College. Now, it was my turn to make an impression on Phyllis's family. She was like a mother hen looking after her chicks. She checked my shirt and trousers to be sure they were clean. She had me polish my shoes twice, combed my hair, and looked over my fingers to see if my nails were clean. I guess I passed the inspection and was ready to greet her family. The whole family: Dad and Mom Burr, Phyl's sister June and her husband, Frank, Dave, Phyl's brother, and wife Carol were at the station, and with fear and trembling, I faced my in-laws. All went well and I soon felt like part of the family. Mother Burr took Michael in her arms but couldn't hold him for long as he was a husky little boy. Grandpa Burr took Michael and you could see that he thought he was okay. Once again,

Michael was passed from one to the other without any protest from him. He soon got to know his Grandma Burr and other members of the family by name.

Michael started to cry, as he was very tired after a busy day. We had a bedroom with a double bed and a baby crib, and again, as soon as we laid Michael down, he was asleep. We weren't long following Michael, but before we could crawl into bed, we had to remove several baby clothes and gifts from family and friends. Of course, Phyl had to look over everything before she was ready for bed.

April 14, 1953, little Rhonwen LaVerne (Burr) King was born. Great Grandma Shuttleworth baby-sat Michael while we were at the hospital. Mom Burr was so pleased to have been there to see the baby born and to hold her granddaughter. I stayed with Phyl all night and every day for five days before we were able to bring her and the baby home. Rhonwen seemed so tiny and fragile you were almost afraid to hold her, for fear she might slip out of your arms. As before, Phyl didn't have enough milk to satisfy the baby and we had to feed her formula in a baby bottle. I told Phyl that I would give Rhonwen her bottle every evening, about 11 o'clock, so that Phyl could get some much-needed sleep. No matter how much or how little I gave her, and how much I burped her, she always managed to bring it up over my shoulder.

By mid-May, it was time for me to get back to Eston. The church board had arranged with the Bible School for us to live in the only building (boy's dorm and laundry in the basement, girls on the second floor, kitchen, dining room, classroom and a bedroom on the main floor) on the School property. There wasn't much cleaning to do as the students had left things pretty clean. Invitations from the Pastors I had written started to come in. A letter from Veteran Camp invited Phyllis and me to take part in the camp Missionary Day. Dad asked his friend, Johnnie James, to drive me to Swift Current to pick up Phyl and the two babies. I noticed a big change in Rhonwen as she had grown so much while I had been away. She was a fat little dumpling and full of smiles. One could see that Michael loved his little sister. We got settled in and contacted a few more pastors for meetings. It seemed as though everything was falling into place for our return to Upper Volta.

I had to borrow my Dad's car to get to the Camp. The Missions Day went well, but a couple of days later, Phyl was not feeling well. I drove her to Coronation where there was a hospital, and we got to see the Doctor. Phyl was running a temperature, and the Doctor wanted her to stay at the hospital, as he wanted to have some tests done. A couple of days later, the Doctor said the tests showed that she had typhoid fever. That meant that she would have to be isolated.

The Alberta Health Division made the Veteran Board thoroughly disinfect the camp and made them postpone a Children's Camp till it was done. Notices were sent to all those who had been at the adult class that they must be inoculated against Typhoid. Michael and I got our three shots as quickly as we possibly could. The Doctor said that I could take Phyl back to Eston and the hospital there, but every time I came to get her, she had a high fever, so the Doctor said she would have to stay. I had to get my Stepdad's car back to him as he needed it for his job. We decided I should go and take the babies with me. Phyllis, uneasy about me driving alone and looking after both Michael and Rhonnie, wanted me to stop at the farm of a friend, Al Ness, and see if he would follow me in his vehicle. It was just on supper time when I arrived and I was invited for supper and to spend the night.

Mom Ness washed diapers and made formula for the baby. I was hanging the diapers on the clothesline when I heard Al arrive in his pickup and held Michael until he had parked. He always parked in the same spot, and as he started a conversation with me, I set Michael down and continued with the diapers. Then I heard Al start his truck and I looked to see where Michael was. He was standing in front of the vehicle and as Al moved ahead, I yelled for him to stop. I ran to grab Michael, but it was too late and I watched in horror as the front wheel ran over his tiny body. Not knowing what was happening, Al backed up and ran over Michael a second time. I ran to him and picked up his lifeless body. Holding him in my arms, I prayed to our Heavenly Father to restore him to life or give us the grace we would need to endure.

I must have been in a state of shock, as that was the last thing I remember. I knew I was put in the back seat of a car, and it seemed like we drove for miles. I learned later that they had picked up Michael's body and driven it to the Funeral Home in Coronation. I heard Al ask me if I would go with him to the hospital, as he wanted to tell Phyllis what had happened. I knew this was going to be the hardest thing I would ever have to do. I didn't know how Phyl would react when she got the news. Would she blame me for his death?

Would she say I should have held Michael until Al was out of the vehicle? Would she say I should have left that evening for home? All this was going through my mind as he drove to the Hospital. In her room, we had to stay just inside the door as she was still in isolation. As Al told what had happened and that it was Michael who had been run over, I will never forget the look of anguish on her face. I am sure she was in shock. She didn't cry, but she seemed to look past us and said: "Oh my God!" I wanted so badly to run over to her, take her in my arms, and console her as best I could, but I couldn't run the risk. As long as I still had little Rhonnie to care for, I had to stay free of typhoid. All I could do was pray for her as we left. I would be going back to be with wonderful friends but I had to leave Phyl all alone in her sorrow.

ALONE? NO! NEVER! JESUS WAS THERE! Had He not said He would never leave us nor forsake us? After the accident, Phyllis wrote to her family: "…Knowing those who are close to us have shared our burden and loss does help in a measure to ease the pain; though for a while it seems it is something one has to go through alone, drawing only upon the strength and grace of the Lord. I can truly say the Lord has been my sustenance and help—a very present help in time of trouble. Every morning, though, as I wake, the realization that our dear little Michael is gone comes fresh upon me, and my heart aches with it, as you can understand. I think a mother's love must be the deepest love this world knows…The Lord knows that my arms ache to hold our little one again, and that is why He sends the balm of His sweet Presence and His precious Word to ease the loss."

I brought little Rhonnie to the hospital so her Mom could see her through the observation window, wondering whether it would cause more pain to see her without being able to hold her. It seemed to lift her spirits for the moment anyway, but so hard when we had to leave. In my devotions I had just read Matthew 16:24: "If anyone desires to come after Me, let him deny himself, and take up his cross, and follow Me." Individually and together, we had committed our lives to Him. Was this one of the crosses we were to "pick up" to follow Him?

Many passages from the Word had taken on new relevance for us—The Lord giveth and the Lord taketh away; God doeth all things well; a very present help in time of trouble; I shall go to him, but he shall not return to me. The hardest we both found, was I Thessalonians 5:18: "…in everything give thanks; for this is the will of God in Christ Jesus for you." So, in this loss, we had to, and by His grace, we did thank Him; for there are no mistakes with the Lord, and what He did, He did according to the counsel of His own will. Someday we might understand His purpose in taking our little one home at such a tender age.

Nevertheless, for the time being, the loss was hard to bear. We would always miss our little Michael, and a part of our lives would always be "away". It seemed rather strange that the first chorus that Michael liked should have been "A way far over Jordan, we'll meet in that land, oh won't that be grand," and he would sing "away" and wave his little arm. The second verse of that chorus starts, "If you get there before I do…"

The next day I had gone back to Veteran camp to await the arrival of my Mom and Dad with my sister, Bess, and her husband. Arrangements for the funeral were being made in Eston. The Doctor had said that if Phyl's temperature remained down they could take her Eston. The only problem was that the Doctor at Eston said it would be hard to find a room where she could be kept in isolation. The Eston Union Hospital had recently burned to the ground, and the Legion Hall had been temporarily turned into a hospital, so space was limited. Because of the funeral, he said he would try and find a place but after the funeral, Phyl would have to be moved elsewhere. My sister, Bess, and her husband, Glenn, opened their home in the country to us. My sister was a registered nurse and quite capable of looking after Phyllis and caring for little Rhonnie.

Sunday morning, Al and his wife drove to Coronation to pick up Phyl, then down to Veteran where Gladys Nicholls was looking after the baby. Bess and my Mom took Rhonnie, and I drove my Dad's car. It was hard to realize that in another car following behind, was the body of our dear little boy in a white casket. His body was with us, but we knew that little Michael was with the Lord, enjoying His wonderful Presence. When the Lord walked upon this earth, how He loved the little children. He took them in His arms and blessed them, and rebuked His disciples for interfering, for He said: "...of such is the kingdom of Heaven." The hymns for the funeral were "Safe in The Arms of Jesus," and "Does Jesus Care." They sang, also, the little chorus that Michael liked so much, "Away Far Over Jordan," and our Pastor sang "The Love of God." His message was to assure us that the death of Christ on the cross covered these little ones that they might go directly into His Presence. Phyl wanted to be alone during the service and said it was wonderful, the peace the Lord gave. She had asked, though, that when the rest went to the cemetery, Sister McLean, our Pastor's wife, come to be with her. She was such a lovely person and was so comforting and helpful.

As soon as the funeral was over, Phyl, Rhonnie and I moved in with my sister, Bess. We still had to take great precautions to disinfect everything and boil her dishes. She was so happy to be able to see the baby again. Rhonnie was growing so quickly and was such a beautiful little girl, but Phyl couldn't hold her for another week.

Michael, October 4, 1952

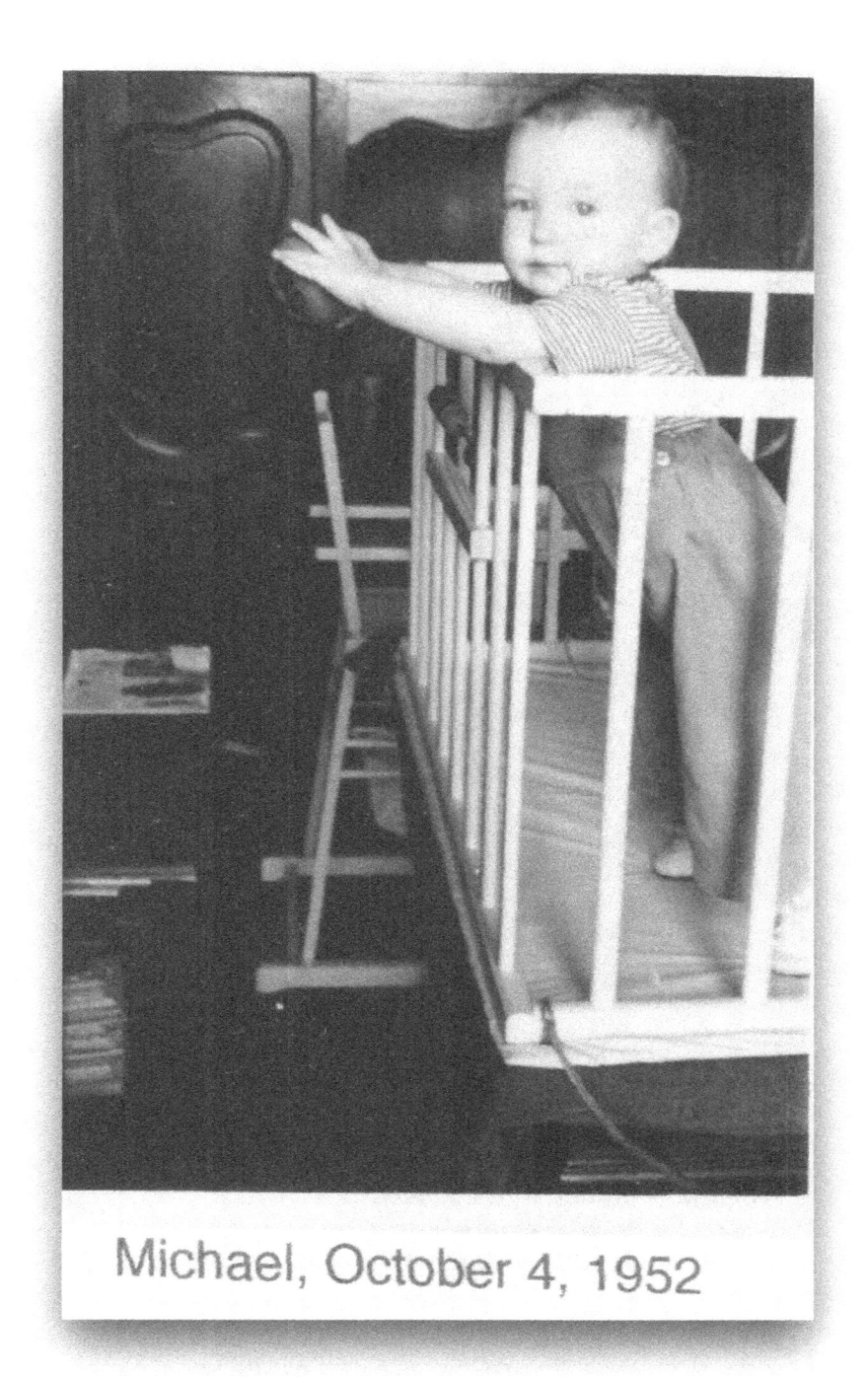

October 31, 1952 "Not content until all the books are pulled off the shelf, and then he's interested in them no longer."

Chapter 21
AFRICA STILL CALLS

WE HEARD THAT PEOPLE WERE WONDERING IF WE were still planning on going to Upper Volta. There was no question in our minds that God's call was still to go, but a lot would depend on what the Eston Church Board felt. If the church was willing to support us as before, we would begin as soon as possible to arrange for meetings to help raise funds for the equipment we still needed, and for our fare. In the meantime, we would spend some time at the Coast with Phyl's family.

The Tabernacle was putting the finishing touches on its Missions Policy. The requirement of the Field Counsel—that new candidates take some professional training—was dropped by the Tab. I was not mechanically inclined, and although I might not have been able to rebuild a motor, I did know which end of the spark plug fit in the block! The Tab had cleared the way for me to be accepted as a candidate.

We were invited to attend the closing Full Gospel Bible Institute Convention at Eston, April 9th to 12th. The ministry of Brother Ericson from Duluth and Frank Smith from Portugal was exceptional. After the Convention, we had a meeting with the Eston Church Board, which was very successful. The Assembly assured us they would undertake our monthly support, our fare to and from the field, and be responsible for any buildings we might need for the work. That only left us with equipment to get, pack and ship.

Brother A.D. Marshall, the school choir director, had planned to take the School Choir on tour again this year as he had last year but found himself without a pianist. He literally begged Phyl to join them for the tour. We had intended to start our deputational travels and didn't think we could afford to put them off. But as it was a case of us going or the choir not going, the Choir, Bible School Board and church Board felt it would be reasonable to combine the two. No one involved thought it a good idea to drag Rhonnie all over the country, and the hardest decision would rest with Phyl. To accept would mean she would be separated from her baby girl again. After what she had just gone through, I knew it was a tough decision for her. After much prayer, I also knew she would accept to go. She was always ready to sacrifice her own desires to help meet the needs of others. She reasoned that through the Choir, many young people might be won to the Lord or called to attend the School to prepare to serve Him. It meant Phyllis or I would get the opportunity to share at each service.

Before we joined the tour, Grandma Hunter had a little birthday party for Rhonnie who'd just turned one. Friends of the family, Katie and Les Howe, accepted to look after her for us during the tour. At the end of the tour, they were pleased to be able to say that she had taken her first steps alone, and that she was potty-trained.

We fared extremely well financially as God undertook for our needs. We had much more exposure with the tour than we would have had on our own. At the end of the tour in mid-May, we applied for visas and were able to book passage on the 'Scotland,' leaving Montreal on September 21st and arriving in Liverpool on the 28th. We also booked to leave Liverpool on October 9th on the 'Apapa' for Takoradi, our entrance point for Upper Volta. We received a phone call informing us the 'Apapa' was full up to that date, but that in special cases they could make a room available. If we wanted it, we were to cable back immediately $260.00. With that settled, we had our reservations complete.

What we needed now was to finish packing our equipment at Eston and ship it to the coast. At the coast, we wanted to buy and pack the rest of our equipment, mostly food items, by the first week of July, as I wanted to be back on the prairies for the summer camps if possible. Phyllis and Rhonnie would stay with her folks at the coast until just before we would leave for Montreal.

After summer ministry and some tearful "good-byes" at New Westminster, it was off to Eston. It felt so good not being under any pressure to meet deadlines, but to relax for a few days. Everything went according to plan and after more "good-byes," we arrived in Montreal with a few days to spare. Our crates had been shipped, the fares confirmed and all we had to do now was relax and enjoy. After arriving in England, I flew to Paris to get some equipment for the field. After my return, Phyllis flew to Dublin to get some information on a Burr Castle her Dad thought was near Dublin. The travel agent couldn't find a "Burr," but did find a "Bir" Castle, about 70 miles from

Dublin. Phyllis didn't have enough time to check it out but did say how much she liked Dublin and the countryside.

On October 7th, we boarded the 'Apapa' on the first leg of our trip to Upper Volta. The first two days on board were very rough, as the boat had been pitching and tossing and rolling from side to side, ever since leaving Liverpool. Poor Phyl was having a rough time as she was sea-sick those first few days. Rhonwen and I were faring well, though, and never missed a meal. The steward promised that tomorrow and thereafter we would be in calmer seas.

Chapter 22
THE ENEMY STRIKES AGAIN

On Tuesday, October 9th, we arrived to the Canary Islands. We'd been looking forward to getting off the boat and taking a tour of the Islands. I must say that physically, I did not feel like going as I was starting to feel ill, but I was thinking Phyl wouldn't want to go if I didn't. But finally, I had to tell her I needed to get back to the ship. I felt feverish, had a bad headache, and didn't feel like eating anything. When Phyl got back from supper and was putting the baby to bed, she said I was lying in my berth looking very feverish. She had asked if I wanted the ship's doctor to come and I'd said it wasn't necessary as I probably just had the flu. But by bedtime, I had such a horrible headache and seemed to have such a high fever that she decided to call for the doctor anyway. He gave me an injection of something and some pills to take as he said he thought I had a terrible cold. Phyl said she was very surprised the doctor hadn't put me right away in the ship's hospital as it seemed glaringly apparent that I had far more than a cold. She said I was burning with fever and could hardly endure my headache or for anyone to touch me.

By morning I was delirious, not making sense, and moaning in pain. I could only remember certain things from that point on. Phyl said she was so frightened that she called the doctor, and he was just as frightened. He asked me if I was stiff in my back and the back of my neck, and when I nodded, "Yes," he had me taken at once to the hospital, while Phyl and Rhonnie were confined to the cabin until they could do some tests. There was an American pathologist on board, and he thought I could have polio as there had been an outbreak of polio in eastern Canada.

I vaguely remember two African sisters and a nursing sister from Hill Station Hospital sitting with me, keeping me cool with cold compresses. Apparently, I seemed to improve on the ship after going to the hospital, although my terrible headache kept up and nothing seemed to help me get to sleep. The doctor told Phyl that she would definitely have to prepare to disembark at Freetown, that there was a good hospital there with a competent doctor (it turned out he was an alcoholic). Phyl was, of course, quite concerned as she faced getting off the boat in a foreign country, with a one-year-old baby, not knowing anyone. However, our Lord had everything planned. A couple who sat at the same table as Phyl in the dining room, came to the cabin door to say that they had contacted an Assembly of God missionary couple in Freetown, who were willing to take Phyl and the baby into their home. Brother and Sister Hemminger were at the dock to meet them.

I recall being let down over the side of the ship on a stretcher and put in a very old rust-bucket; a waiting ambulance. Sitting in the hot sun, it was like an oven even though the two sisters brought cold compresses to make the wait more tolerable. I was unconscious by the time we got to the Hospital and very heavily drugged. Phyl had gone to the hospital to pray with me, but after prayer she left because I was unconscious. That evening, the doctor called for Phyl to come to the hospital, as I was still unconscious but having severe convulsions. He said I was not a pretty sight, but that if she wanted to see me alive, she would have to come now, for if I lived until the morning I could very possibly be in a vegetative state. The nurse in charge took Phyl to the isolation building and left. I was bound to the gurney and padded so as not to hurt myself; my tongue was tied so I wouldn't choke, and I had been bringing up and foaming at the mouth. Phyl wrote later to our parents: "Oh, dear ones, if ever I had to draw on the Lord's strength, it was then...if ever I felt the battle with the powers of darkness, it was that night!"

Sister Hemminger had said that if Phyl wanted to stay at the hospital for the night, she would look after the baby. Phyl stayed, and in the middle of the night asked the nurse if she could pray for me. The nurse was perfectly willing, and after a few minutes she let her in. Phyl wrote: "I tell you, our dear Stan was in the very jaws of death!" She said she prayed for the Lord's divine healing touch, but if not, she would sooner He would take me home than for me to live the rest of my life out of my mind.

I was unconscious all day Sunday and had several small convulsions. Monday morning when Phyl received the call from the doctor, asking that she come to the Hospital, Phyllis said she expected the worst and that it must be that I had passed away. The doctor ushered her into the ward and there I was, sitting up and drinking a cold glass of tropical juice! The doctor seemed almost apologetic that I had regained consciousness after he had said he didn't think I would make it through the night. The doctor wanted her to come immediately as he thought I might have a relapse and not recover. However, Phyl and the other missionaries could not help but feel that the Lord had seen me through.

Phyllis had sent cables to both the Tabernacle and Eston churches on Sunday. The Tab had received theirs just as the people were leaving, so a special prayer meeting was called for later in the afternoon. Over 70 people came to pray. The Eston church service was already over when the cable arrived, but people were contacted by phone that afternoon. Because of the time difference between Freetown and the churches, I gained consciousness and started to improve even as they were praying.

We later found that many people from churches in many countries were also praying. That very Sunday, when things looked hopeless, God was answering prayer. The Matron, and a couple of other nurses, who at the beginning said they could give Phyl no hope that I would recover, seemed almost embarrassed now. They said it would take a miracle, and now that a miracle had happened, they seemed reluctant to believe it. Well, praise the Lord, a miracle had happened and all in answer to prayer. How we praise Him for faithful, praying saints!

I never lapsed into unconsciousness again but steadily improved. I was not able to focus properly yet, and I found it hard to follow Phyl if she spoke too fast or said too much. I spoke very slowly but was completely rational. As I slowly got my strength back, I was allowed to sit up, and soon was able to walk around without too much trouble. I was moved to the main hospital and a day or two later was overjoyed to be allowed to spend the days at the Hemmingers' with my wife and daughter. I did have to return to the hospital for the night.

My visits to their home, however, were short-lived as I was confined to the hospital once again. A huge, very painful abscess developed on my left hip. For almost a week, with the help of poultices, it drained the most horrible looking and foulest smelling discharge imaginable. The doctor said it was my body clearing out all the toxins that had built up in my system.

Phyl, Lucille Davies, and Gordon and Marg Lungren would be calling at Freetown on December 11th on their way to Takoradi. The plan was that we would travel together to Takoradi and then on to Leo, arriving in time for Christmas. We were grateful to the Lord for a letter from Jack Gordon, informing us that our equipment shipment from Vancouver had arrived in Takoradi and had been forwarded on to Leo.

We started getting our baggage together for when the 'Accra' would arrive in Freetown. However, once again our plans would change! Whether another attack from Satan to try to end our ministry in Africa before it had even begun, or whether it was another cross the Lord was asking me to take up and bear, or both, but December 1st I woke early in the morning and found I had lost control of my bodily functions and that I was paralyzed from the waist down.

The doctor was at a loss to know what could have been the cause. Over the next ten days, he had several blood tests done, but they revealed nothing concrete. The thing causing the most concern, was the fact that the three doctors on the 'Apapa' had diagnosed my trouble from the beginning as TB of the spine and decided it had now reached the area of the spine and was causing meningitis. The Doctor at Freetown said he suspected the same thing. The x-ray machine had been broken, but when it was repaired, he told me the results were very suspicious as there were cloudy areas in the lung. He thought there must be a focal point of TB somewhere. Not knowing the reason for the paralysis, and therefore not knowing how to treat it, the doctor said he would discharge me as soon as we had passage booked back to Canada. Being so close to the land to which the Lord had called us, we asked the Eston church and the Field Council for permission to stop over in Upper Volta on our way back to Canada. Permission was granted and after 5 1/2 weeks, I moved from the hospital and joined my family.

Phyl and Rhonnie had been staying at the Brethren Missionary home right in the heart of downtown Freetown for several weeks now. The James' had said they would like to help us as well and give the Hemmingers a break. The daily temperature was about 85 degrees and getting hotter, but very humid which made you feel sticky, with your legs feeling like lead. Little Rhonnie was doing fine and never seemed to slow down! She was such a sweetheart. It was cooler at the Brethren Mission because of the breeze off the ocean, and we would have much more room. The Hemmingers had been so good to us; Mr. Hemminger had driven Phyl almost daily to see me at the hospital, and he and Mrs. Hemminger looked after Rhonnie for us. They and their churches certainly helped sustain Phyl when she was going through such a difficult time.

It felt great to be home with my wife and baby girl. I was still having dizzy spells, especially when tired, and my vision still blurred. My sense of balance was poor, and I staggered when I tried to walk. We had to pack our excess baggage (some we had brought with us from Canada, and others we had purchased in England and France on our way through England) and have it delivered to the port. I was limited in what I could do so most of the work fell on Phyllis. She was able to take the baggage through customs, ready for it to be picked up when the 'Accra' arrived.

As the 'Accra' glided into the dock, we drove down. Phyllis had a boarding pass so went on board to meet the two families. I wanted to go onboard too, but while walking across the dock using only a cane, I fell, banging up my knees, and had to be taken back to the Mission. The folks on board hadn't gotten our letter about the paralysis and were terribly disappointed when they heard we wouldn't be continuing on with them. They agreed that to travel with them and make the 600 mile inland trip would be too much for us. The Eston Church Board had said they were not in favor either and urged us to take the plane.

Brother Hemminger drove us to the Brethren Mission where Mrs. James had prepared a delicious noon meal. At 4:00 p.m., he drove them back to the ship. The new arrangement was that we would fly to Bobo Dioulasso in Upper Volta and that the Davies would meet us there on December 28th.

We had a few things to do to get ready to leave in two week's time. There had been a lot of washing, ironing and packing to do as well as Rhonnie and "Dadda" to look after, so, poor Phyl didn't have much time to relax as most of the preparations depended on her. We were up rather late the night before Christmas, as we spent the evening with the James'. Being of Norwegian descent, they opened their gifts on Christmas Eve.

Bobo Dioulasso Airport, 1958
Martin & Alice Davies (2nd row, left of centre)
Stan & Phyllis King (centre, wearing hats)
Lucille Davies and Daniel Davies (son of Martin
 & Alice, in suit jacket), Rhonnie King (age 5)

Chapter 23

THE DAY HAS ARRIVED

WE LEFT FREETOWN ON THE 27TH AS PLANNED. Phyl had to handle the check-in at 6:30 a.m. and I was taken to a launch on a baggage cart. The Hemmingers, the James', the 7th Day Adventist missionaries were all at the dock to see us off. We were incredibly grateful to the Lord for them, as they'd had a big part in my recovery by their prayers, their visits, and their care and concern for Phyllis. We all prayed as we parted and wondered if we would ever meet again, sorrowed by the fact we doubted we ever would.

After a half-hour ride on the launch, we had a long way to walk to the bus, so they loaded us onto a hand baggage cart and wheeled us over. We then had a very long ride on the bus. I don't know how they could call it the Freetown airport; it was so far away! We had to sit and wait until about 11:00 a.m. as the plane was almost two hours late. We flew from there to Monrovia, Liberia, which was on the coast directly south of Freetown. We were taken from the airport by taxi to a French restaurant for dinner. About 2:00 p.m. we departed and made two more stops before reaching Bamako where we would stop for the night. The two stops were short, but all the passengers got off the plane. Because of all the steps involved in getting on and off, I chose to remain onboard. The plane was quite comfortable while in the air, but sitting on the tarmac under the hot sun, I thought I would roast as it got just like an oven!

Phyllis was not feeling very well before we arrived at Monrovia and continually got worse. No doubt fatigue, the heat, and the pressure of getting ready for the move, were all part of the reason. I was able to look after Rhonnie after supper and Phyl was able to get a good night's sleep. She was fine the next day, thank the Lord!

At 7:00 p.m. we arrived at Bamako, and while everyone else walked, they gave us a ride to a bus on the baggage truck. We were then taken to the Grand Hotel and were surprised to see such a ritzy place in the centre of West Africa. It was large, with a foyer in the centre and two large dining rooms. On one side there were tables on a patio with an orchestra in attendance and on the other, a particularly good restaurant. We had a large room on the 1st floor, with a bath and a private balcony. It cost us about $10.00 for the night.

We were booked to take a DC3 plane, the same type as the previous day, from Bamako to Bobo Dioulasso. The DC3 is a freight-passenger plane and not at all comfortable to ride in. The seats weren't fancy and didn't recline. We asked to have our reservation changed to a DC4 that was leaving at the same time. Instead of three stops and a four-hour flight, we were non-stop to Bobo in 1 hour and 10 minutes. Praise the Lord!

Baptismal service at the marsh (Boura?) Phyllis & Rhonnie seated under upturned boat for shade, 1950's

Chapter 24
History of Upper Volta/Burkina Faso

Burkina Faso is a landlocked, flat country in West Africa about two-thirds the size of Saskatchewan, with a population estimated at over 20.9 million, according to a 2020 census. The capital, Ouagadougou, has a population of just over 2,200,000. The country became a protectorate of France in 1896, and later, for administrative convenience, it became part of three other colonies. In 1947, it once again became a separate colony named Upper Volta after the three tributaries of the Volta River—the Black, the Red and the White, that have their source in the country.

In 1960 the country became independent but maintained a close relationship with France. A civilian government was elected and in 1966 it was overthrown by the military; corruption, among other things, was given as the reason. For the next 50 years, the country saw one military coup after the other, corruption listed among the causes for the takeovers. In 1984, one of the military leaders determined to eliminate corruption, changed the country's name to Burkina Faso and its inhabitants' name to Burkinabe, which means *People of Integrity*. In 2014, a popular uprising forced the last military leader to resign, and in a free and fair election, a civilian government took control of the country.

Burkina Faso is a multiethnic nation with more than sixty linguistic groups; French is the official language. The literacy rate in Burkina is about 35%. The French encouraged the writing of the different languages and dialects of the country and also literacy programs to teach the people to read and write their own language. As much of this work has been done by missionaries and mission organizations, many of the people now have access to the Bible--individual books, the New Testament, or the whole Bible.

The tropical country is divided into two zones: the northern zone, the Sahel—adjacent to the Sahara Desert, and the southern zone—the Savannah. The tropical climate has a wet and a dry season. In the south, the wet season lasts from May to October and receives more rain than in the north. However, rains vary greatly from year to year, in both timing and quantity. The rains generally arrive with violent winds and severe thunderstorms. The vegetation varies with trees and thick brush in the south and near-desert conditions in the north. The landscape changes dramatically according to the seasons. In the driest months, extreme drought, the Harmattans (dusty, hot winds of the Sahara), along with widespread, manmade bush fires, dry out almost all vegetation. With the first rains, leaves sprout on trees and bushes, and beautiful flowers emerge as if by magic, only to quickly disappear. Elephant grass begins to grow and within a few months, it will reach a height of 8 to 10 feet (240 to 300 centimeters).

Burkina Faso is one of the poorest countries in the world with few natural resources. The great majority of people engage in subsistence farming. The principal exports are cotton, gold, and shea nuts harvested from the Karite tree (the oil and "butter" is high in vitamins, minerals and amino acids and is used in cosmetics and soaps). Early crops in the wet season include peanuts, corn, yams and rice, while sorghum and millet, both staples, are harvested one or two months into the dry season. Cattle, sheep and goats are raised. Large numbers of young Burkinabe migrate to the coastal regions of Ivory Coast and Ghana to work on the coffee, cocoa and banana plantations. The annual income is estimated at $1,000.00.

In sub-Saharan Africa, one in every six children (160 per 1,000 live births) fails to reach his or her fifth birthday. The most dangerous time in a child's life is the first 28 days after birth—when over a quarter of all child deaths occur. Life expectancy today in Burkina Faso is 62 years but when we arrived in 1954, it was only 30 years!

Burkina Faso has some of the most diverse wildlife in West Africa with more than 650 mammal species. Some of the most common land animals include elephants, buffalo, hippos, monkeys, baboons, lions, giraffes, warthogs, hyena, leopards and various species of antelope. When we arrived in 1954, these animals were abundant. Some local hunters had rifles, but most had handmade flintlock guns, that were as dangerous out one end as out the other and were fired from the hip. The natives used poison arrows that would kill an antelope with just a scratch, yet the meat was safe to eat. The French administration began issuing permits for long guns almost upon demand. It wasn't many years until most of the wildlife had disappeared. Even in the game reserves, poachers, working with the game wardens, were threatening many of the animals with extinction. Our mission kids, Clark and Carol Lungren and Robert and Eleanor Lungren, turned things around on the Nazinga Game Reserve. With the Government providing new game wardens they were able to drive out the poachers. After studying animal habitat and food, building dams for water, and gaining the confidence of the villagers living around the perimeter of the park, they were able to reintroduce the missing antelope and see them thrive. Other animals followed. Unfortunately, after the Reserve became profitable for the Government, the two families were unceremoniously kicked out of the park.

Crocodiles thrive all over the country in rivers, marshes and dams. As in most cultures, they are sacred and must not be killed. Various species of fish are also found in the same water sources. Geckos, lizards, chameleons, hedgehogs and scorpions are found throughout the country. Vigilance is necessary at all times as venomous snakes—vipers, mambas and cobras—are everywhere. Other reptiles include the non-poisonous rock python and the boa constrictor. Over the years there had been 16 children on the mission, but thanks to the Lord's protection, only one child had ever been stung by a scorpion and not one bitten by a serpent.

Little did I realize the role that this impoverished, land-locked country would play in my life after I first heard of it while a student at FGBI.

Clark Lungren driving jeep. Stan in back with friends. Possibly on the Nazinga Ranch….

Chapter 25
ARRIVAL IN UPPER VOLTA

NOT KNOWING THE REASON FOR THE PARALYSIS, and therefore, not knowing how to treat it, the Doctor said he would discharge me as soon as we had passage booked back to Canada. Being so close to the land to which the Lord had called us, we asked the Eston church and the Field Council for permission to stop over in Upper Volta on our way back to Canada. The plane made a smooth landing at the airport in Bobo Dioulasso and on the evening of December 26, 1954, Phyllis and I stepped out onto the soil of the country to which the Lord had called us nine years ago. Jack Gordon, one of the founders of the Upper Volta Mission, was there to meet us.

After pounding over some of the worst roads in Africa, we arrived at the mission station of Silli, the home of the Gordons. Every year the missionary families met at one of the mission stations from Christmas to New Year's for fun, fellowship and games, as well as to deal with business relative to the work in each area. As the Gordons were hosting that year's get-together, we were able to get acquainted with all of the mission families in a very short time.

Crippled, dragging my legs, with Phyllis holding our year-old daughter, it wasn't the arrival on the field we were expecting. Having reached our goal, would we be able to stay? If we returned home, would we ever get back? We were invited to stay as long as we wished, to see what would be best for me.

From the Gordon's to the Davies' mission station, I was to ride in the back of the Hildebrandt's pickup. I was wearing a light short-sleeved shirt and short pants; what seemed to be the required attire for Africa. Before we arrived at Leo, I was afraid I would freeze to death! Hot Africa? Not for three months of the year, I learned, when cold winds from the desert sweep across the country. I assure you, when we returned to Upper Volta after our first furlough, we brought back some winter attire!

Phyl Davies, a senior missionary, had prepared a place for us at Leo. Our shipped baggage had arrived from the port of Takoradi, Ghana, where, in September, we were to have been met by Jack Gordon. Our accommodation consisted of two medium-sized rooms, with a small room for the wood-burning stove, and a bathroom about six feet behind the dining room.

For the next few weeks, we went through all the protocols as new missionaries, even though there seemed to be no improvement in my condition. A couple of months later, we accompanied the Davies to Bobo where I was able to get an appointment with a French Army Doctor. After a complete examination, he said that he would be able to get my legs working again in a matter of months.

Arrangements were made for us to stay with Eldon and Luella

Johnson at Diebougou; the closest mission station to Bobo. Every morning for three weeks, a male nurse from the dispensary would give me a Vitamin B12 injection. With the shots and much exercising, my walking did improve to the point where, within a few months, I could manage with only a cane.

Chapter 26
STORMS OFF THE SAHARA

WE HAD TO GO TO OUAGADOUGOU, THE CAPITAL city, for supplies as there was very little available in the bush during our early years. The first thing on our list of things to do was to get money from our bank account and buy the provisions we would need while in the city. On this particular trip, as I neared the city, there were inky, dark clouds forming along the horizon and I knew there was going to be a wicked storm later on in the morning. I was praying that I would be able to get everything done before it hit. There can be destructive, hurricane-force winds that can cause damage to the aluminum roofs and blow down the huge trees that line the streets. I went to the bank, only to find that there had been a reason to close the bank during the morning hours. I was urging God to hold back the storm until I could get back to our guest house, but everything seemed to be moving at a slow pace. After I got my money, I had to take time filling the car with gas as I was getting extremely low. Again, another wait as many drivers had decided to do the same. I handed my list to the grocery store owner's son, and before I completed the list, his Dad came in and had to do some business with him. Already the wind was starting to twirl the leaves and dirt on the streets, and I knew I would not be able to beat the storm.

My heart sank and I began questioning the Lord for either not holding back the storm or for allowing it to take so much time to get my business done. The streets of the city are lined on both sides with huge Caicedra trees which had weathered many a storm. It wasn't long before I saw the wind blow down the first tree, fortunately, or by the grace of God, in the opposite direction to the street. Ouagadougou has a well-known film festival and to advertise it, banners are stretching across the road from tree to tree. On the end of the banners are pieces of wood like our 2X4, about 3 feet long. Some of these had detached and were being whipped around by the wind. It had already begun to pour down sheets of rain, making it almost impossible to see. I had to wait until the end of the banner had hit the ground before I dared try to pass it. The pieces of wood were heavy enough to do serious damage to the vehicle. Part of the road went through a wide section of a storm drain for these heavy rains. On both sides of the road there were bicycles, motor scooters, even several of the light French, Citroen cars, blown off the road.

Our guest house is at the back of the Assembly of God (AoG) Mission on the western end of the city. There are two entrances: the first for the Church lot, and the second for the Mission. I could see from a distance that a huge Caicedra had fallen across the first entrance and that another had blown over across the second entrance. There was no way I could get back to our guest house.

500 meters up the road was a compound where I knew Timothy, our farmhouse boy lived, and I knew I could shelter with him. A half-hour later, the storm with all its outrage and fury had passed. I drove back to the AoG yard where men were out with chain saws cutting up the trees so vehicles could pass. I told the Mission Director that I had tried to get back from town before the storm. He replied, "It's a good thing you didn't, as a huge tree has fallen and demolished your house!" I drove back, and sure enough, the roof of the central sitting, eating, kitchen area, and the bedroom/bathroom on the right side was crushed by the tree. Right where I had almost always sat when doing accounts or typing letters a heavy branch had broken the table. I had to apologize to the Lord for grumbling about all the delays in reaching the house. My life had been spared by those delays, by the grace of God. One bedroom had been spared, so we were able to use that while the rest was being repaired.

Chapter 27
FILLING IN AT KASSOU

THE HILDEBRANDTS, AFTER RETURNING FROM their first furlough, had begun to build their home in Kassou; a new area. However, as Helen was expecting their second child within a few weeks, Field Counsel asked Phyl and me to move to Kassou. We were to help with the building and also continue visiting the nearby villages with the Gospel. Armien had gotten permission from the local administrator for us to live in a large, round grass-roofed hut, used by Government officials on business visits to the area. The walls were about 3½ feet high with the roof supported by pillars every eight feet. The grass roof had recently been replaced and leaked like a sieve when it rained. We would sit in the center of the bed under a plastic tablecloth thrown over the mosquito netting, until the rain would stop. The grass roof created a daytime hiding place for bats and lizards, and it was not unusual to see where a snake had shed its skin during the night. In the morning you'd tap your shoes to make sure a small snake or scorpion hadn't taken up residence. Many times in the morning, we would find frogs in our shoes who'd sought a good shelter for the day. At dusk, the bats by the hundreds would vacate the roof in their search of insects. Because of the continuous droppings from the roof dwellers, I had to make a ceiling of aluminum roofing sheets that covered our table and the kitchen counters and cupboards.

The hut was about a kilometer from where the house was being built. The only vehicle available to us was a 1½ dual-wheeled Chevrolet truck that had been sent from supporting churches to help with the building projects on the field. It was extremely rough riding, required much maintenance, and was heavy on gas—which was very expensive. I bought a bicycle as I found I could ride a bicycle much easier than I could walk, even though I had lost much of my sense of balance.

While the Hildebrandts were away, I had the use of Armien's pick-up. My first job was to crib up a well on the edge of the marsh with small stones and cement. One morning, as I prepared to crawl down the well, I saw a double row of sharp teeth and two beady eyes staring up at me. During the night, a crocodile had fallen into the well! Not knowing what to do, we called for the village chief and elders to come and remove the croc. They had workmen try to put a rope around its neck, but all efforts were in vain. Armien and I discussed shooting the beast and dragging him out. When one of the workmen heard of this, he warned us that it would create a serious problem with the village. The crocodile is considered sacred and the life of each crocodile was in some way related to each person in the village, in such a way, that if the crocodile dies, that person will also die. If we killed the croc and someone in the village died, the mission would be held responsible for that person's death.

That night, Armien saw that a storm was brewing, and dug channels from the higher ground down to the well. It poured rain for an hour and continued into the night. In the morning, the well was full and the croc had disappeared. God had helped us out of a situation without the beliefs of the people being offended.

After the well was finished, we collected rock for the foundation of the two bedrooms to be added to the existing room. While the Hildebrandts (or Hilds), were on maternity leave, it was my job to build the foundation and the walls. The rocks were very heavy, and my legs were still weak and would get so tired and sore I could no longer ride my bike back and forth, so we moved into their home. In the evenings, I kept going to the bush villages for meetings. I wondered how much of the Gospel was getting through to the people though as we were using young school kids, with only a few years of primary school, as interpreters.

Armien was driving an older model Chevy pickup for which spare parts were not always available. The diaphragm for the fuel pump had already been changed many times with plastic cut from a car seat cover. Coming back from a bush meeting, the motor stopped and I knew it was the fuel pump. As it was too dark to work on it that night, my only recourse was to walk home.

The next afternoon, and with a very poor plan of attack, I set off on a motorbike to change the diaphragm. I am not sure about the distances involved, but about a kilometer from the vehicle, the moped stopped and nothing I could do would get it to go again. I had brought a thermos full of water but on a hot, humid day, it was soon gone. By the time I had walked to the vehicle, I was exhausted and my efforts to get the fuel pump working were unsuccessful. There was nothing to do but set out on foot back to Kassou. I was so thirsty I wondered if I would make it back. I berated myself for not having worked out a plan to have someone come looking for me if I didn't show up at a certain time. Phyllis was unaware of what was going on and so was not concerned. All I could do was cry out to the Lord for strength for each step. It was on my mind that many wild animals were roaming the bush at that time of the evening. By God's grace I stumbled into a hut where we had left some provisions. A tin of apple juice never tasted so good!

In January of 1956, the Hilds were back with little Raymond. As I had finished the foundation but hadn't been able to do more, the next several days were spent building the walls to roof height. I asked the Field Council if we could take an early furlough, as both Phyllis and I felt exhausted. They decided we should try to stay another year and begin a project that we would be able to promote when we did return home.

Inside our round mud house with thatched roof

Our home-Kassou, Fr. West Africa, July 1955

One of the classes of Bible School students with instructors Armien Hildebrandt, Stan & Phyllis

Church Leaders & Missionaries
Armien Hildebrandt, Jacques Ziba, _____, _____, Jacques Nignan, Gord Lungren, Marc Zalve, _____, _____, Abraham, Stan

Chapter 28
We Choose the Sissala People

On our way back from Bobo, after seeing the Army Doctor, we had stopped to visit the Paramount Chief of the Sissala people at the village of Boura. During the conversation, the Chief asked if Phyllis and I would be the couple to move to Boura to build a mission station. His words struck a note with me and a few days later, I mentioned it to Phyl. She said immediately that she, too, felt the same way. After much more prayer, we told Field Council that we were sure the Lord wanted us to work among the Sissalas.

There was a permanent primary school at Boura, and the remains of the old, mud school were still standing and seemed to be the only livable place in the village. Of the three rooms, only one had enough of a roof to give us adequate shade from the sun during the day. At sundown, the ubiquitous bats by the hundreds, took off in black clouds, seeking their evening meal of insects. We loaded our few belongings into the mission truck and in January 1956, we were settled in the old school and began the work of building a more permanent home.

As the mud bricks we would use for our home were the same as the people used for their homes, we hired local men to do our building. The mud bricks were made in the marsh and transported by truck to the building site. Other building materials such as cement, lumber and aluminum roofing sheets, had to be purchased in either Gold Coast or Ivory Coast, and shipped north by truck for pick up. Thank the Lord, I was always able to find all I needed just across the border with Ghana, saving a lot of driving miles.

The sun goes down in the evening around six o'clock and there is no twilight. Every evening when too dark to work on the house, I would cycle to several compounds to share the Gospel, taking a schoolboy or two with me to interpret. Once a week in the late afternoon, I would visit two or three nearby villages, traveling in one direction one night, and later in the week, the opposite direction.

Phyllis was also busy with daily classes for the school children, as our yard bordered the schoolyard. She had a girls club for older girls who showed a greater interest in spiritual things. She also held meetings for the ladies, making it sound more special by stipulating that no men were allowed. Rhonnie was of special interest and no doubt a drawing card, as she was the only white child most of the people had ever seen.

Finally, the house was finished to the point where we felt we could move in. We packed up and moved a few of our things to the house, but Phyllis thought it would be best for us to spend the night in the schoolhouse. I could see a storm building up and we could only pray that the storm would pass us by. However, about midnight the storm struck. The roof leaked everywhere and our only protection was the plastic tablecloth that had served us so well while living in the hut in Kassou. Early in the morning, I heard a clapping outside and I knew someone had a message for us. It was from the Chief, informing us that over half the roof had blown off our house.

As Phyllis was still sleeping, I drove to the house to assess the damage. I had tried to hold down the roofing sheets with heavy cut stones, but in the hurricane-force winds, that was not sufficient. The rocks that had fallen had bent the frame of our bed, smashed Rhonnie's tricycle and her bed, and punched big holes in the cement floor. Everything was covered in a layer of mud. I hired two men to begin the cleanup while I drove to the schoolhouse to face Phyllis, not knowing what her reaction would be. But as stoic as ever, as we hugged, she said, "Thank the Lord we hadn't tried to move into the house last night."

The first order of business was to drive into Tumu to buy the needed roofing sheets. It meant we would have to spend a night or two more in the school. As the roof was made with small branches in layers of clay, now that the clay had turned to mush, large gobs of it were falling, and we knew the roof could give way at any time. Two days later, we moved out of the school and settled into our first house in Upper Volta, in the middle of the Sissala people whom we believed God had called us to serve many years ago.

As life expectancy is only around 55 years, funerals are quite common events. We were invited to attend the funeral of one of the Chief's relatives. Sacrifices were offered to the village and family idols, and that was followed by music and dancing. The rhythmic playing of the balafon, the beat of the drums, the swirl of the flutes and the singing, are all meant to excite the people to the point of going into trances. We watched as they carried an elderly lady out of the hut and sat her on the ground. It was evident that she had guinea worms and could not walk.

The guinea worm parasite is found in unfiltered water, such as marshes or shallow wells. The parasites carrying the larvae are released in the stomach and migrate to the intestines, where they grow up to a length of 100 cm or more. The females move to the skin, usually on the feet or lower leg, and form a blister from which they emerge, discharging the larvae. The openings generally become infected causing swelling, ulceration and intense pain.

We watched the old lady as the music got louder and louder and the dancing more and more intense. Suddenly, she threw aside the tattered shawl that covered her top, stood to her feet and began to dance; slowly, at first, and then increasing her speed until she was pounding the ground ferociously. She stopped suddenly, fell to the ground, and was carried off into the hut. As we continued to watch, we both began to realize what we were up against in trying to reach these people with the Gospel.

There was plenty of work to do besides increasing our village outreach. I started to make plans for a permanent house. This meant many trips to the bush for rock for the foundation. After getting part of the foundation in, I realized our mud house would not survive until a permanent house could be built. We decided to build a smaller building in which we could live and which could later become a garage, storeroom and a guest room.

While in Ghana, I had seen two men making bricks under pressure with a hand machine. The bricks were made of clay with a couple of handfuls of cement, and just enough water to moisten it. Then, with the push of the lever, they were compressed. The bricks seemed very solid and were certainly cheaper to make than the cement block the mission was using up until then. Unfortunately, I wasn't able to find one for sale at that time, so that project would have to be put off until after furlough.

Both Phyllis and I now felt completely exhausted and no longer able to carry on the work. At the Christmas gathering in 1956, we asked for permission to leave on an early furlough. It was decided that the Lungrens, who were soon returning from Canada, would take over the Sissala work. We had poured our love and our life into reaching as many Sissala people as we could with the Gospel. The people had captured our hearts but had broken them as well; as up until then, none of them had accepted Christ.

Rhonnie with one of her vervet monkeys, 1958/9

The day we left Boura, three young school kids, around 10 to 12 years old, came to the door and said they wanted us to know that they had accepted Jesus as their Saviour. One small ray of light amidst so much darkness.

The children's ministry, Boura, 1963
Rhonnie, back centre
Marc Zalve, back right

The house in Boura being built

Making mud bricks for our first house in Boura

Chapter 29
Searching for Answers

Despite the three kids and their confession of accepting Christ, we went home discouraged. Was the darkness in which the people sat so great that even the light of the Gospel couldn't penetrate it? We struggled with that and even considered asking permission to go to another field. However, wiser heads advised us not to rush into any decision until later in our furlough.

My home doctor lost no time in searching for answers as to what could have caused the sickness on the boat. As it had affected every part of my body from my feet to my esophagus, appointments were made with specialists, who tried to find answers. The conclusion was that I'd had meningitis and encephalitis; none were sure what had caused the paralysis. I was told not to expect too much change in my condition, but that efforts would be made to improve each problem as much as possible. Among the operations, there was one called "Fundoplication" which was to narrow the opening between the stomach and the esophagus. Stomach reflux had already damaged the esophagus beyond repair, so there was still the lurking possibility of a ruptured esophageal wall. Although the Lord had saved me from the jaws of death, He chose in His divine wisdom, to leave me with several infirmities that exist to the present time. Many people, all in good faith, have prayed for my healing, but the Lord's answer to me is always the same, "My grace is sufficient for you..."

In the meantime, we were trying to determine what we should do after furlough. We both knew we had been called to Upper Volta and could point to the very day and hour. The Lord began to show us Scriptures that would help us with our decision. We'd had a glimpse in Kassou, with the crocodiles, and in Boura, with the women dancing at the funeral, of what we would be facing if we returned. We knew it was the god of this age that had blinded their eyes to the truth. Even as was the Apostle Paul's in Athens, our hearts were burdened when we saw the whole country given over to idols. Our purpose in going to Upper Volta was to see the people turn to God from idols; to serve the living and true God (1 Thessalonians 1:9).

We both felt the Lord was speaking directly to our hearts when God spoke to Paul in a vision: "...do not be afraid, but speak, and do not remain silent; for I am with you, and no one will attack you to hurt you; for I have many people in this city." With encouragement from our Pastor, many Christian friends, and even most of our families, we decided to return. So it was that in March 1958, we left Canada for Upper Volta, with the approval of the Field Council to return to Boura. The Eston church had taken on the full support of Phyllis and me, which meant any funds we received while visiting the churches could go directly into the work. Phyl's Dad, who was not a Christian at that time, was not happy with our decision, and blamed me for taking his daughter to what he called "that God-forsaken hell-hole."

Deputation, 1958

Return to Africa-Takoradi, April 1958

Chapter 30
A NEW BEGINNING

EVEN BEFORE WE WERE SETTLED BACK IN OUR Boura home, we began services. Phyllis started classes again with the school children and the women. Just before nightfall, I began visiting the near-by villages that surrounded Boura, and later, as darkness descended, I switched to the compounds that made up the village of Boura. The Lord directed me to concentrate more on the village of Yoro. The Yoro chief had confessed Jesus as Saviour under the Lungren's ministry, but had returned to his Muslim faith because of his fear of offending the supreme chief of the Sissala people.

The chief was eager to have us come to his village and invited us to have our weekly meetings in the village compound where the village idols were kept. We had an idol house behind us, and a cylindrical mud idol about 8 feet tall on either side of us. The blood and flour sacrifices made to the idol gods for the village were seen at the very top of the idols. As we were singing amidst all of the village idols, I was reminded of the words of David, when he wrote, "I will praise you with my whole heart; before the gods I will sing praises to you." (Psalm 138:1)

After several months of sharing the Gospel, I felt it was time for the people of Yoro to make a decision. For over an hour, they were asking what they would have to do to become Christians. Their prime concern was their responsibilities towards the idols of their ancestors. Finally, they said they would give us their answer the following week. I can assure you we were much on our knees in prayer. When I say, "We," I generally mean my interpreter and perhaps some young Christians who came along to help, especially with the singing. It was difficult for Phyllis to come with us because of Rhonnie. It was already dark; the road was in extremely poor shape with a long, rickety bridge to cross and snakes of all breeds out for their nightly hunt. As Phyllis had her classes during the day with the children and women, and Rhonnie's school lessons, she remained at home. Of course, there was also the evening meal to prepare while I was away.

At last, came the moment of truth. What was their response to be? Imagine my utter disappointment, when not one person showed up at the meeting place. They had made their decision to remain with their idols, rather than follow Christ. We waited in case there was maybe even one who had decided for Christ. The village of Yoro is divided in two by a huge marsh and just as we were ready to leave, a man arrived from the other side of the marsh. He said he had been sick and when he had let us pray for him, he had been healed. We decided right then to move to the other side of the marsh and begin the meetings there.

When a French school opened in Leo, a young man from Yoro, Souana, working in Leo, applied and was accepted. This led to him getting a job in Leo. The missionaries at Leo were impressed with him and led him to the Lord. When baptized in water, he took the name Pierre. He started well, but when visiting some of the villages, because of the stature of his family, he was offered wives by the other village chiefs. According to the Scriptures, this disqualified him as an evangelist, but it didn't prevent him, as a Christian, from sharing the Gospel. He worked for the Government, and then retired to his village to farm with his sons. He, Pierre, was the family chief of the compound in Yoro where we were going to begin holding meetings.

Enroute to Lan, July 1955

Chapter 31

God Confirms the Preaching of His Word

There was a good attendance each Friday night, with people coming from the nearby villages. One evening when we arrived, the men were all sitting out in front of the huts looking so glum. Pierre said they were waiting for us so we could pray for one of the women who had been in labour for three days and still hadn't given birth. They led Abraham and me into a dark room, lit only by the flame from a clay saucer filled with oil. As my eyes became accustomed to the dark, I made out the form of three women.

One lady was lying naked on the floor with the other ladies each holding one of her arms. A large log lay in front of her. I looked for signs of her breathing but could see none. Was she already dead? These two women had been dragging the young mother on her stomach over the log, trying to force the baby to be born. Both Abraham and I prayed for the woman, then we went out to start the service. Shortly after, there was a lot of commotion, with women coming and going. Pierre informed us that everything was all right now—the baby had been born, although dead, and the mother was up and doing fine. The people who had come for the service from

Yoro and near-by villages were all talking excitedly. Later, Pierre told me they were all so moved by such a demonstration of power. The news soon circulated, and we had Chiefs coming from several villages to our door, asking if we could come to their village to tell them about the God of such power. "Where can we find such power as this?" they exclaimed. "Our idols do not have it!"

We now began to understand why, during our first term, there had been no response to the preaching of the Word. They were not ready to give up what they had for something they were not sure about. Once God began to confirm the preaching of the Word with signs and wonders, then they were ready to respond. Unfortunately, we were already visiting all the villages we could work into our schedule, but we did try to make at least one visit to each village. How we needed to train workers to teach the Word of God! In all of the areas of our field, some young Christian men had been spiritually nurtured in the Children's and Youth classes. These men were now ripe material for Bible School training.

The Boura Chief with his number one official wife, Disetta (1980)

Chapter 32
BIBLE TRAINING CENTER

SEVERAL YOUNG MEN WERE WILLING TO GO BY bicycle to some of the villages, but it took much of my time trying to help them prepare Gospel messages each week. Besides trying to reach as many villages as I could, I was also busy trying to build a more permanent residence for ourselves. Our mud house was showing signs that it could soon be falling down around our ears. At times, Phyllis and I felt overwhelmed by what needed to be done, as we realized the enormity of the task of reaching all the villages in the area. We found the same was true of all of the other areas of the field. The Lord impressed on our hearts that the answer lay in a local training program for our youth. Up to that time, we had sent a small number of promising young fellows to an American school in a neighboring country, but distance and expense made this impractical.

At the Christmas Mission Conference in 1961, Phyllis and I presented our conviction that a Bible Training Center of our own was imperative. After much discussion and waiting on the Lord, the decision of the Conference was unanimous in favor of launching out on this project. The larger village of Leo was chosen as the most suitable site, and Phyllis and I were asked if we would assume the responsibility of raising funds for the necessary buildings, draw up a curriculum, and that I direct the school.

This meant that Phyllis and I would have to leave Boura and our work among the Sissalas whom we had come to love, and move to Leo. We were not happy at the thought of having to leave the work where we had been seeing a recent move of the Holy Spirit. After much prayer and discussion, we decided we should make the move. The Lord impressed on us that by training young people for the ministry, we could multiply our ministry.

Early that summer we left Africa for a year's furlough, and during our time in Canada, presented our vision and the financial needs for the school. Our hopes and plans met with enthusiastic responses everywhere, and the Assemblies supporting missionaries on the field promised financial help. Once again, the Eston Church stood back of the work of the Lord in this need, and later, more than fulfilled its pledge of financial support. We returned to the field with sufficient funds to build a residence for the Director of the School, and a dormitory to accommodate 3 married couples on one side and up to 10 single students on the other side.

We moved into temporary quarters in Leo while building the house, which took almost two years to complete. Even before the house was completed, a class of four illiterate, prospective Bible students gathered five days a week around a card table on the verandah where Phyllis launched them into Beginners French. The Bible School Classes would have to be in French, as there were several languages and dialects spoken throughout the mission.

French was also the official language of the country.

I started taking classes with two young fellows who were eager for classes to begin: Marc Zalve and Jacques Nignan. I had to know what level of French they could understand before I could begin composing material for the first-year studies. In November 1966, the first Bible School class convened. Eight students worked in temporary quarters in the mission guest house where two bedrooms were turned into classrooms. They were divided into two classes—Phyllis's class being for those who had little or no French, and mine for those who could read and write some French.

At the end of the term, our hearts were filled with joy and thanksgiving unto the Lord, for that which He had accomplished in the lives of these students. It was a great encouragement to see the spiritual progress they had made, and with what zeal they returned to help in the work of the Lord in their home churches.

Construction of Bible School House

One of the Leo Bible School Buildings

Boura-July 24, 1960

Circa 1960

Chapter 33
Extended Furlough

As well as working with the Bible School at Leo, we continued our work among the Sissalas, driving back each weekend and visiting as many churches as we possibly could. During the Bible School terms, the students were able to gain some practical experience by accompanying us on these trips.

In 1967, we returned to Canada on an extended furlough due to family matters. As it was felt the Bible School was too important to leave unattended until we could return, the Field Council invited Armien and Helen Hildebrandt to move from Kassou to Leo, to take over the operation of the school. Now the Hilds faced the same dilemma we had—do they leave the work at Kassou where they were absorbed in a period of most extensive outreach in their area and move to Leo to teach a handful of students? Since four of the students were from the Kassou area, they realized that promoting their development was the higher priority.

At that time, Bob and Zell Paterson were new missionaries on the field and stationed at Leo. Bob worked with Armien to build another dormitory and a building with two classrooms and a chapel. Armien spent long hours at night, preparing notes for the following day's classes; Bob taught part-time. As the student body increased, new staff members were needed. A Nuna national and accredited teacher, Isaac Diasso, joined the staff for two years. Other nationals were called upon to help, as well, and many of the other missionaries gave their time.

Upon our return, we took over the Bible School again, as well as the ministry among the Sissala. In Boura, a whole family—father, mother, and two boys—accepted Jesus as Savior. The mother had two brothers living in the village of Bouyaque. The sister, Marie, begged me to visit her brothers, as one of them was interested in the Gospel. Etienne had joined the French army and served in France, where he was first exposed to the Gospel. Now, discharged, he was back in his village and wanted to know more. His village was about 25 kilometers away and only accessible by bicycle.

Abraham and I had to leave Boura at around 5:00 a.m. to get as far as we could while it was still cool. There was a good number from the village waiting for us when we arrived. Because of the interest, we arranged with the villagers to come every other week. After a few weeks, we noticed that Marie's other brother was now coming to the meetings. It wasn't long before several men had accepted Jesus, and soon they had constructed a mud Church.

On the way to Bouyaque, we passed through one of the compounds of Goumou, where an elderly man was always waiting for us. We took the time to share the Gospel with him each time. One day, he invited us in and said he wanted to show us something. Sitting in a corner was a young lad, maybe 13 years old, who the father said had been working in the field when all of a sudden, he had become paralyzed from the waist down. He was devastated, as he only had one son to take care of him. We prayed for the son every time we went through the village. Phyllis and I left on furlough without seeing any change in the boy. Before we left for home, we helped install one of the Bible School students, Samuel, as pastor of Bouyaque, and supervisor of the surrounding villages.

Not long after we returned to Canada, we were overjoyed to hear that the lame boy had been healed. He was baptized in water and took the name of Daniel. There was soon a church started in the village.

Isaac Diasso, Clementine & family, Leo, 1980

Bible School Students
Boura Church Pastor, Abraham, on far right

First year Bible School Students at Leo, 1966
Leo Church Pastor Jacques Ziba in front centre

Stan and Abraham baptizing a new convert. Abraham later became the Pastor of the Boura church.

Stan and Abraham on left at a baptismal service. Phyllis on right playing the accordion.

Chapter 34
YOUNG MEN WHOSE HEARTS GOD TOUCHED

SAMUEL HAD ATTENDED A YOUTH CAMP AT LEO AND had accepted Christ as his Saviour. He lived with his family in the village of Ti, where I was having meetings regularly. He was continually faithful there and seemed to have a good grasp of the Scriptures. He always wanted to help so I asked him if he would take a class with the kids, while I spoke to the adults. The kids can be quite a distraction, running in and out during the message. However, when I would arrive, I would find he had already had the meeting with the kids. I got more than a little provoked at Sam until I found the reason he took the children early was so he could get in on the message to the adults. Sam was one of the best students at the Bible School, and no matter where he was placed, he always left his churches stronger than when he came. At present, he serves not only as President of our churches mission wide, but he pastors a church, with great help from his wife, Martine, in Bobo. He also oversees three other churches in the city, as well as primary and secondary schools and a College. There are several satellite churches he is in charge of also, including a missionary church in the neighboring country of Mali.

From Phyllis's ministry, many school kids and village kids were being saved. As young as they were, the Lord was using them to spread the Gospel. A man came to Boura from a village about 15 kilometers away on an afternoon when Phyl was having a children's service. Afterward, he told Phyl that he wanted to hear more and that he would come Sunday mornings. He first got interested by hearing one of the school children in his compound talk about Jesus. Because of the children's faithful witness, the man became a Christian, stopped offering sacrifices, and got rid of all his idols.

We realized the illiterate village kids needed more training than what they could receive in their home churches. It was decided that we should have a School where the students would be taught Bible, French, and carpentry. Gordon Lungren took on the project and it proved to be a great success. Martin Davies took over and added more trades such as cement work, furniture making, and roof building. Eventually, under Gordon, it became mostly furniture. As the program grew, a carpentry teacher was hired, and a classroom, a dormitory for the students, and a residence for the teacher were built. Many of those students who went on into the ministry were able to support themselves through the trade they had learned at the Trade School.

One of the best students at school chose the name Marc when baptized. He graduated from primary school and was eligible to go to Secondary School. This meant that at 13 years of age he would be in the city, more or less on his own, where there were endless temptations—alcohol, cigarettes, drugs and more. Sad to say some of our kids, while in the city, got in with the wrong crowd and no longer walked with the Lord. I asked Marc if he would consider going to Bible School for one year, hoping this would strengthen him spiritually while away from home. He consented, much to the disappointment of his family. They had hoped he would continue his education, get a good job, and help support the family. At the end of the first year, I asked Marc if he now wanted to go on to secondary school, and very emphatically, he said no, he wanted to continue at Bible School. Young as he was, he became my interpreter and a particularly good pastor. In the meantime, his family became Christians and, much to their credit, supported Marc and his ministry. While in Bible School, Marc felt the need of being baptized by the Holy Spirit. In his fourth year he was getting desperate, and in the middle of the night he went alone to the chapel and poured out his heart to God. Before he realized it, the praises he was offering to the Lord were in a different language. This experience made a profound change in his life, and in his ministry in the years to come.

During the summer months, the young Bible School students generally went back to their villages to cultivate. Many got involved in preaching the Gospel, and several churches were founded. Marc and I tried to supervise these churches and mentor the young pastors. And so the Gospel spread; people getting saved, baptized in water and many being filled with the Holy Spirit.

Mission homes being built

Abraham Katou Matthieu Jacques Abel Philippe Abraham Sou

Chapter 35
BIBLE TRANSLATION

I FELT THE NEED OF HAVING THE SCRIPTURES IN THE Sissala Language. Two young German ladies, with Wycliffe Bible Translators, were working on the Sissala language across the border in Ghana. They were approached to see if they would be interested in working on the language in Burkina. They consented, but one of the ladies decided to remain at Leo and work on the local language there. The other lady, Regina, moved to Boura and chose two of our Pastors, Marc and Luc (a young Bible School student who had founded several churches) as her informants. The team made a good beginning—until Regina left on furlough. She left strict instructions that no one was to use her work while she was away. Later, she decided to stay in Germany for two more years to get her degree in Linguistics.

As we did not want to wait two or three years longer to begin the translation, I went to see the head of Wycliffe in Burkina with a proposition. I suggested that since Marc had learned the basics of translation, that he be allowed to present a manuscript for the language specialists to examine. They were incredibly pleased with the work and said it was one of the best manuscripts they had ever received. His work was so good, that Wycliffe eventually hired Marc, sent him for more training, and he became one of their manuscript reviewers.

It is one thing to have a Bible in the language of the people, but it is another to have people who have learned how to read. A young schoolboy called Nicolas came to know Christ in Phyl's children's meetings, and at age 13 came to Bible School. He was highly active in Evangelism and was soon overseeing several churches. Wycliffe sent out from Canada a language specialist, to train young men and women to learn how to read, and how to teach the newly written language. Nicolas turned out to be one of the best, and along with his wife, Jeanne, was soon training others to teach. By the time the New Testament was completed, there were around 1,000 people able to read. Some pastors invited all who could to come an hour early to church to hear the Scriptures being read. A para-church organization made cassette tapes of the New Testament and made players available for those who hadn't learned to read. So powerful was the effect of having the New Testament in the local language, that shortly after Phyllis and I retired from the field, we heard that every Sissala village had a church.

In 1999, after Phyllis and I had retired from the field, we received a letter from Marc informing us that the Sissala New Testament had been printed and was due to arrive by boat from the printers in September. Phyllis and I would have loved to have been there, but Phyllis had come home because of an illness and was not able to travel.

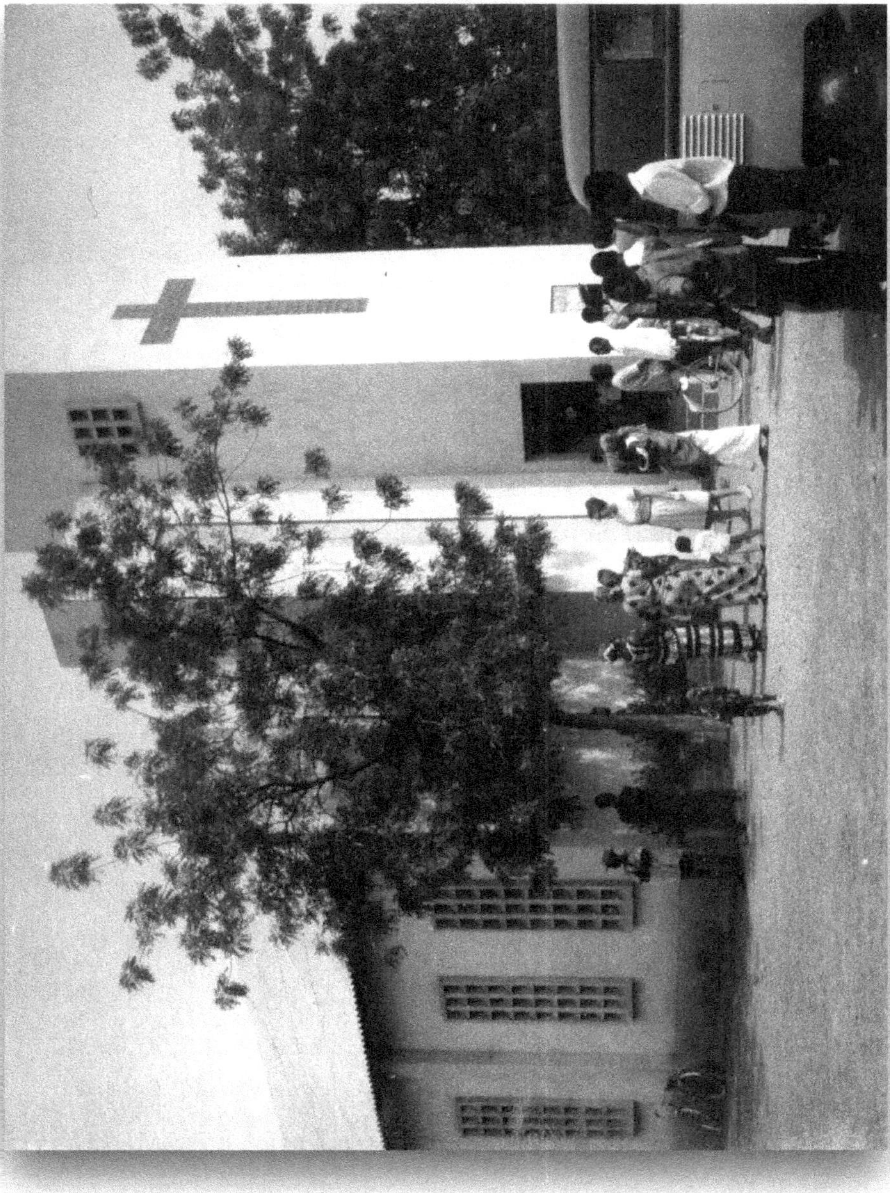

Chapter 36
OLD THINGS HAVE PASSED AWAY

As soon as possible after Phyllis and I got back from furlough, I wanted to visit the church in Goumou which had started after Daniel was healed. On that day, Christians had come from several of the surrounding villages, so, as there wasn't room for all in the church, we held the service outdoors. As I was about to speak, a woman from the nearby village of Boufian said she was sick and asked for prayer. After we had prayed, I felt urged by the Holy Spirit to close my prayer by exhorting her, "Sin no more, lest a worse thing come upon you." I must confess, I never thought anything more about the woman until two or three years later when I was teaching at a weekend gathering of Christians.

During testimony time, a woman told of how she had gone to Goumou when I was there and asked for prayer as she was not well. Her husband was Muslim, and she had tried all that the Muslim teacher told her to do, without success. Her husband urged her to offer the sacrifices the witch doctor required, again without success. Her husband then told her to go to Goumou; that the white man would be there, and that is when she asked for prayer. When she was healed, she told her husband they had to become Christians;

otherwise, a worse thing would come upon her. Several people in her village accepted Christ and a new church was formed.

Luc, Marie's brother, continued to attend church at Bouyaque. I was able to visit the church there only once a month, and on that day, Luc was waiting for me. He testified that after many months of listening, he was convinced that to accept Jesus as their Saviour was the only way he and his family could be saved from sin and assured a place in Heaven. He wanted me to come to his home and break down all his idols. We made a date, and on that day I brought with me several of the Bible School students. Luc gave me his hoe and led me into his house where there were several figures made of mud, stained with blood and flour where he and his family had offered sacrifices to the spirits. I refused the hoe and told Luc it was better for him and his family to smash the idols themselves. That way the devil would not be able to turn him from Christ by convincing him that nothing had changed as he hadn't broken the idols himself. Once the idols were broken, we carried them out and pulverized them, and began a search of the house for all the fetishes he had collected over the years.

The Sissala religious beliefs are based on animism, the belief that spirits can inhabit inanimate objects such as trees and rocks; fetishism, the belief that an object can be given magical powers which can benefit or injure humans, such as an amulet to protect a newborn baby; and totemism, the belief that an animal, plant or other natural object is ancestrally related to an individual or family, and must not be eaten or killed by members of the family, such as monkey meat or scorpions. Fetishes can be anything that has been given power by sacrifices ordered by the Witch Doctor. The most usual sacrifice offered is a chicken. The Witch Doctor will slit the throat, and for several seconds the chicken will flop around. It must land on its back to be accepted by the spirit, but if not, chickens must be sacrificed until one does. The fetish will then be hung in the house along with the other fetishes.

You can imagine all the fetishes hanging in Luc's house that his family had accumulated over the years. These were all piled together and set on fire. Luc then produced a little carved wooden doll, and I knew that Luc had been a twin.

Twins are considered an evil omen, and one of the twins must die either by natural causes or human intervention. The mother must pay the Witch Doctor to have a wooden doll made to replace the dead twin, and it must never be separated from the living twin. It was a real step of faith to see Luc have his twin doll thrown into the fire.

The next place to rid of fetishes was the rooftop where a large canary was used to hold small stones gathered out of the fields. As the farmer cultivates his field, and his hoe strikes a small stone that catches his attention (it may spark, jump, or move unusually) it is believed it is a spirit that wants to be friendly. It is placed in the canary on the rooftop. We began throwing the rocks in every direction from the roof, and noticed people fleeing from the village, fearing the wrath of the spirits. When nothing catastrophic happened, they returned to their homes.

The next step for Luc was to be baptized in water. This meant a walk of 2 miles to the nearest marsh. The spirit of the Bouyaque Marsh was reputed to be one of the strongest for miles around and people came from all over to offer sacrifices for the spirit's help. It is full of crocodiles and no one dares to enter the water without first having offered sacrifices to appease the spirit. When we arrived, Luc, some of the Christians, and I entered the water and people were scurrying away, afraid of what the spirit might do to the intruders. As nothing seemed to happen, many stood by to hear Luc's testimony, many hearing the Gospel for the first time. Luc's obedience in getting rid of his idols, not only strengthened his own faith, but also that of the churches as well.

Chapter 37
The Power of the Enemy

A man from Bouyaque went south to work on the plantations in Ivory Coast. Years later, he returned home, and to make a living, started killing the crocodiles in the marsh. The village elders warned him that if he continued, the spirit of the marsh would punish him. He said he didn't believe that anymore because while in the Ivory Coast he had converted to Islam. A few days later, while riding his bike on the path beside the marsh, he fell to the ground paralyzed on the right side. The elders again warned him that the spirit of the marsh had punished him, and that the village idols would strike him next. A few days later in the village of Bouyaque, going past the village idols, he fell off his bike and died.

The Government sent trucks from Ouaga to bring back loads of yams and other produce from Leo and Yoro, for the schools and Colleges in the city. Because the roads were in such a horrible state, the Government hired a French firm to build bridges across the many marshes, in preparation for putting through a new road. Near Kassou is a stream and a marsh called the Pandi. The bridge there, as were most bridges, was made of large poles holding up large cross poles. Smaller branches were placed over these poles and several inches of mud on top of that. Early in the rainy season, the dirt washed away leaving the bridge unusable. The workmen came, put up the wooden forms for the foundation and the pillars, poured the cement, and left for a couple of days. When they came back and removed the forms, the concrete crumbled away. They rebuilt the forms, poured the concrete, and again left it a couple of days. Again, when they removed the forms, the concrete crumbled; this happened three times. The third time, an old man was working at the marsh. He asked if they had offered any sacrifices to the spirit of the marsh. Of course, they hadn't, and the old man told them they would never succeed until they did. They went to the Witch Doctor in the closest village and offered chicken sacrifices until three chickens in a row landed on their backs. The workmen put up the forms once again, poured the concrete, and came back in a couple of days. Once again they took off the forms and found the concrete solid. They were able to go on and build the bridge.

Yearly Bible study and fellowship weekends became immensely popular with the Christians. For the first few years, the missionaries picked up the Christians from the villages around where the conference was to be held that year. Generally, a missionary and a native pastor were invited by the host village to take the Bible studies. Friday afternoon I was taking the service at the village of Lon, when an elderly lady said she had been sick for days and wanted prayer. With the church elders, I prayed for her healing. Saturday morning the same lady was back and said she had not been able to sleep and was still not feeling well. Again we prayed for her. By the afternoon she was feeling worse than ever. One of the elders asked her to take us to where she slept. She always slept in the same place on a natte that is rolled out at night and rolled up in the morning. She indicated the spot where she placed her natte. The elder began searching the ground under her natte, dug a hole, and pulled out a cloth in which some of her hair had been wrapped. Someone had put a curse on her for some reason. We had prayer for her healing and the evil spirit was bound and cast out. She was completely healed.

After Bible school closed, many of the students went home to their villages. One student, Zachary, who returned to his home in Boura, told me that he would have to find a new place to stay. His room was built up against the idol house, and he said there was such a racket coming from there at night that he couldn't sleep. I threw open the door and went inside. There were idols made of mud and carved from trees, sticks of different shapes and sizes, stones and other fetishes, and more. All had been given power by the sacrifices offered to the spirits. I asked him how such a collection like that could make such a noise. No one would dare to enter the idol house for fear of being struck dead by the spirits. The villagers were expecting me to fall over dead, and when I didn't, wondered if it might be because I didn't know only certain people had access. Another opportunity to share the Gospel!

A hunter from the village of Poudiene used to pass through our yard on his bicycle on his way to the Chief's compound. He carried his bow and arrows with him at all times. When he came by, if I was there, he would come to the house for a little chat. On the bow that he carried there were two or three cowry shells. These shells came from the Coast and were used as money when we first arrived in Upper Volta. As we were talking, I reached over, took the cowry shells in my hand, and asked what they were for. Immediately he drew back and told me I shouldn't have touched them, as they were fetishes that had been given power by sacrifices offered by the Witch Doctor. He said my right arm would wither up in a few days' time. For the next several days, whenever I would see him, I would wave my right hand. I didn't do it to make fun of their beliefs, but to show that my God was stronger than their fetishes.

Chapter 38
GOD ANSWERS PRAYER

THE MORE THE LORD DEMONSTRATED HIS POWER, the more people were being filled with the Holy Spirit and believing God to answer their prayers. Sissala villages are made up of several family compounds, with the oldest brother being the family chief. They cultivate small crops such as peanuts, corn, or millet around their compounds, but they all have fields in the surrounding bush. Daniel was one of the first converts in Boura, and he quickly developed spiritually. The families in Boura had built a dam across the marsh to ensure a year-round supply of water. During a prolonged drought, it was a constant matter of prayer. On a Saturday, the church called the Christians together for prayer and Daniel was among those who prayed. That afternoon the sky started to darken in the east, and it looked as though rain was on its way. The storm hit in the evening with all the fury of a tropical downpour, and in the morning the people awoke to water; water everywhere. The rains had washed away the dam and all roads out of the village were covered as well as all the crops in the low-lying land. At church Sunday morning, Daniel was on the hot seat as it was, because of his prayer. In his prayer he had asked three times for the Lord to send rain, now the Christians were jokingly saying, "Daniel, the next time you pray to God for rain, just ask once! We don't need this much rain at one time!" Eventually, I was able to get funds through a European donor to build a reinforced dam, ensuring a good water supply for the village.

Elephants and other wild animals roamed at will when we first moved to Boura. The Africans used poison arrows to kill animals for food and occasionally killed marauding elephants. Some hunters made their own flintlock guns which they fired from the hip, as they were too dangerous to fire from the shoulder. Unfortunately, the French Government started issuing long gun permits and in a few years' time, all the animals were killed off or had moved out.

The crops of the farmers were fair game to the elephants. When a troupe of elephants was heading towards where Daniel had his crops, all the other farmers hurriedly offered sacrifices to the Witch Doctor for a fetish to put up in their fields to protect them. Daniel told those of his family and neighbors that he was not going to put up a fetish as the Pastor had said that if we trust in God, He will look after us. As night fell, all the farmers in the area began to beat drums, tin cans, or anything to make a noise in hopes of frightening the animals away. They soon had to retreat to their compounds and hope for the best, as the herd arrived. In the morning, anywhere you looked was utter devastation: the corn crops were flattened, the yams dug up and the peanut crop had disappeared. The only crops that survived untouched, were those of Daniel.

While driving from Leo to Yoro for Sunday service, we saw an old man, Moses, and his young son standing at the side of the road with a large, full sack. The man had worked for years on the plantations in the Ivory Coast, and having lost his job, had returned to his village. He had been able to plant rice in the marsh and had an excellent crop. Every year, at the end of the wet season, the cattle herders set fire to the elephant grass while it is still green at the roots. Saturday morning, Moses had noticed smoke in the air and discovered flames were heading straight for his field. He told me that all he could do was pray. He said he told the Lord, "Lord, you know I am an old man and all I have been able to do is plant this rice crop. If it burns, I will have nothing, but I pray to You to please help me." The flames, getting closer and closer, suddenly changed direction as they neared his crop. The wind had started to blow away from the field, and his crop was saved. He wanted me to take the sack of rice to the church as his thanks to God.

We were surprised one afternoon by the visit of two men from the Christian and Missionary Alliance. They were on their way to Ghana via Leo, to do some shopping. We rarely had anyone drop in like that but thankfully, Phyllis had some fresh-baked cookies to serve with coffee. Just before they left, they asked if there was anything they could get for us while in Ghana. On the spur of the moment we could think of nothing, but just as they were disappearing down the road, Phyllis came running out of the house to stop them, but it was too late. We were completely out of toilet paper; in fact, out of any kind of paper, and had just missed an opportunity to get some delivered to our door. We had a good laugh over it and Phyllis suggested we pray about it. On their way home, the men stopped in again, and just as they were getting in the car to leave, one of them asked us if we could use any toilet paper. They said they had found a good bargain in Ghana and had bought two big cartons. When we told them what had happened, they insisted we take one carton; they would take no payment for it. They said they felt blessed of the Lord to be His means of answering our prayer.

Chapter 39
A Safe Home for Teenage Girls

Not only were many young boys coming to the Lord throughout the Mission, but many young girls as well. Though forced marriages had been against the law for many years, the old cultural practice continued, although mostly in the bush areas. Most of the girls involved were too afraid of the repercussions inflicted by their families to dare resist. Marriages were sometimes arranged before the children were born. Many girls are given as wives to men old enough to be their fathers or even grandfathers. In such cases, the young girls led a miserable life as slaves to the other, older wives. Sometimes the girls would try to run away, only to get caught and be severely beaten.

Two young girls, one from Yoro and one from Kassou, were brought to the Leo Mission Station to escape being forced into such marriages. When we gathered for our usual Christmas fellowship and business meeting, it was decided to build a home for these girls until the churches had developed, and were strong enough to take charge of their own girls.

A dormitory was built for the girls, and a small separate dwelling built for the Housemother and food preparation; all in an enclosed compound. As many as 14 girls at a time have lived in the home, ages ranging from 12 to 19 years old. We were not able to "kidnap" these girls, but if they were able to get to the home on their own, or with the help of others, the families were not able to come and take the girls back.

The girls at the home were kept very busy. They took turns, in pairs, cooking for the unmarried Bible School students, had daily Bible studies, as well as classes in hygiene, childcare, needlework, reading and writing. They had to hunt dry wood out in the bush, as well as gather certain condiments from specific shrubs or trees.

Many Bible School students ended up marrying one of the girls from the Home. How blessed to see these once harassed girls become wives and mothers in Christian homes. Altogether, over the years, at least 80 girls passed through the Home. As the churches became stronger and were able to take care of the young ladies, the last of the girls left the home in 1990.

Safe house women-Leo, Burkina Faso

"Home" girls- Jan. 1989-Note the baby of one of the girls who is married to a bible school student.

Chapter 40

A VISIT TO GHANA

IN 1970, WE RECEIVED A LETTER FROM ACOP Head Office, asking if Phyllis and I would meet with a group of Christians in Ghana. This group, Prayer Group, and Evangelistic Association had heard of Apostolic Missions through a young Ghanaian, Felix Quaye, who had visited Canada, and a lady who had taken many big boxes of used clothes to Accra, where Felix had a Bible School.

After our Bible School at Leo had closed for the summer months, I wrote the leader of the group, Emmanuel Mensah, to set up an appointment for a visit. As I never got a reply, Phyllis and I decided to go down to Accra and see if we could locate them. We stayed in the A of G guest house, but none of the Christians that we came in contact with there had heard of them. We were invited to church Sunday morning at the army camp and were delighted to find a young man who knew the group and who would be able to drive us to Tema, where the group had their headquarters. Emmanuel invited us into his home, while he tried to contact others of the group. The group was made up of businessmen, most of whom were elders from three of the old-line churches—Presbyterian, Methodist and Anglican. They were not happy with the spiritual decline of the churches over the years, to the point that they were no longer Evangelical. They met together once a week on Fridays for worship, prayer, Bible Study and planning for weekend evangelistic meetings in the surrounding towns. Their meetings in Tema were held on a cement slab with poles supporting strips of canvas for walls and roof--not very elegant, but certainly a place full of the glory of God.

Sunday morning, I was invited to speak at a Presbyterian Church. Just last year, the elderly Pastor had been brought back to the Lord through the Prayer Group and had been filled with the Holy Spirit. A few of his congregation of 150 members he knew to be born again. I spoke simply from John chapter 4 showing how religion or church membership are not sufficient to be able to worship God acceptably, but a spiritual new birth is essential. At the altar call by Brother Mensah, a former elder in a Presbyterian Church, the entire congregation responded and came forward. The way of salvation was presented again and they all repeated the sinner's prayer. Eternity alone will reveal all that was accomplished at that time, but the Pastor was elated and so grateful to the Lord. It was an answer to his prayers and preaching; a new beginning for his church.

On the way back to Tema we stopped at the Accra General Hospital to pray for a sick lady. All eight of the other patients in the ward were witnessed to and prayed for. Two young girls aged 13 and 20 gave their hearts to the Lord. The older girl had been watching as we visited the other beds, and when we arrived at her bed, she burst into tears and cried: "I want to be saved!" She was wearing two rings that she had gotten from a witch doctor for protection. Without hesitation, she took them off when asked to do so, and flung them from her. Praise the Lord!

The last Saturday morning I had the pleasure of baptizing 22 recent converts by immersion in Jesus' Name. In the evening I was able to meet with the Brethren who expressed a desire to affiliate with ACOP. They invited me to share the Word with them on Friday and take part in a weekend crusade in a nearby Lory Park (passenger truck stop). Thursday and Friday there was special prayer for the crusade. Friday night there was a crowd of nearly 600, including Christians. Saturday night the crowd had increased to around 800, and Sunday night there was over 1000 present. Altogether, over 100 adults and young people responded to the altar calls and were dealt with for salvation. Their names and addresses were recorded for follow-up work. Many children, also, were taken aside and dealt with by a young lady, Mary, who was active in child evangelism in the primary and secondary schools in the Tema area.

Often there was no evangelical church near to the village where people were getting saved, so sufficient follow-up was very difficult. I proposed to the Group that they become a Church Fellowship and register with the Government. That way they could form churches where believers could meet and receive teaching. They chose to be called: Full Gospel Evangelistic Ministry of Ghana; before long they had several small churches registered. Their biggest need now was permanent Pastors. They'd heard we had started a Bible Training Centre in Burkina, and asked ACOP if they would permit Phyllis and me to start a school for them in Tema. With ACOP's blessing and what we felt was the blessing of the Lord, we consented. After our School at Leo closed for the wet season, we drove down to Tema to start making arrangements for a classroom, recruiting students, and to start preparing notes in English for 1st-year studies.

Two young men from Tema, Samuel, son of Brother Mensah and Joseph, had already had some Bible Training in a "For All Nations Bible School" in Lagos, Nigeria. Their studies were good, and with some revision were usable, which gave us four teachers for the opening of our School. Four young people had applied as students and we were able to rent a public-school classroom.

Each year the number of students increased, but there was no way for the grads to be ordained. Brother Mensah wanted to be ordained and I thought he had all the qualifications for ordination but didn't know how to go about it. Head Office suggested I become a member of Full Gospel Evangelistic Ministry, and as an ordained minister, I would be able to ordain him. Gillis Killam, our home church pastor and Willard Mitchell, a deacon in the church and Business Manager of FGBI, were wanting to visit Upper Volta, and I suggested to Bro. Mensah that that would be the ideal time for him to be ordained if they could also extend their visit to include Ghana.

As the number of students increased yearly, we had to keep looking for new classroom space. We also thought the Bible School should be turned over to the churches as soon as possible, and with the blessing of ACOP, two couples, Samuel Mensah and his wife, Victoria, and Dan Digber and his wife, Janet, were offered scholarships to FGBI. They found the weather particularly challenging, but the Congregation saw to it that they had sufficient warm clothes. They were invited into many homes for meals and fellowship. Both the ladies became pregnant and each gave birth to a son. They became involved in ministry as soon as they moved back to Ghana.

Dan lived in a suburb of Accra, about an hour's drive to Tema and the Bible College. However, as there was no regular bus service, it was often late in the day before Dan could get to the school to teach. While on furlough I raised sufficient funds to buy a motorbike for Dan, but Rev. Mensah insisted it was too dangerous and borrowed money to buy a vehicle for Dan. As Ghana was going through a recession at this time, the Fellowship was not able to raise the borrowed money, so turned Dan's vehicle into a taxi, leaving him no way to get to Tema and the Bible School. He eventually resigned and started his own ministry group.

Tema is divided into communities, and Sammy took over as pastor of the Community One church. As the congregation grew to over 200 (the capacity of the church building), they had to have two services on Sunday mornings. Continued growth meant adding a third meeting in the afternoon. The membership had been fundraising for several years and finally decided they had sufficient to build a larger facility. As the plot of land on which the church stood was all they were able to get from the Government but was too small for two buildings, it was decided the new building would have to be built over top of the old one.

At the church in Tema, Ghana

Gillis Killam, Stan, newly married couple, Willard Mitchell

Page 225

Marc Zalve, Yoro, 1981
Marc was like a brother to Rhonnie. He was one of the first graduates from the Bible College in Leo. He pastored and planted churches among the Sissala. He was a teacher at the Bible College, and then the Vice President. He was involved with the translation of the Bible into indigenous languages.

Marc & Suzanne Zalve, Clement, Aline (children by first wife, Martine) and Caleb Leo, 1980

1980 Christmas Morning Service at Leo Church

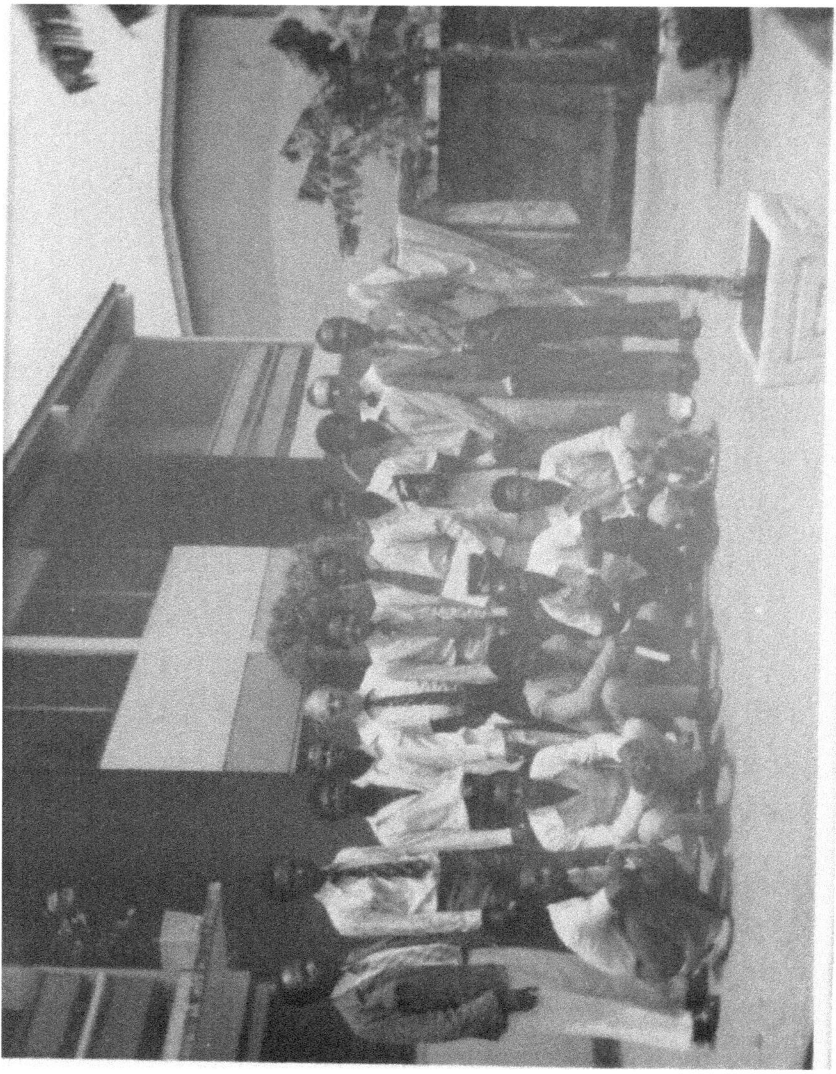

Chapter 41
THE CIRCLE IS COMPLETE

IN 1990, WE RETURNED FROM BURKINA FASO FOR health reasons, after 36 years on the mission field, and took up residence in our own home in Eston; located kitty-corner to the Eston Full Gospel Church. Many ministry opportunities continued to keep us active at the church and the Full Gospel Bible Institute. We had come full circle, but we had left a part of our hearts in Africa.

In 1987, Rhonnie had married Rick Wenden in Australia, and then in 1996, we were delighted when our precious granddaughter, Rhea, was born. They reside in Australia but did move to Canada for a short time in 1998 and 1999. It was a real joy to be able to spend quality time with them during that time.

After about 20 years of enjoying life together in Eston, Phyllis needed to move into Jubilee Lodge for more care. I visited the love of my life every day until Sat. Nov. 24, 2012, when she fell asleep and woke up in heaven.

After Phyl passed away, I began working on my memoirs. There have been countless wonderful times and so many years of events that it has been hard to condense everything into one short book. I relived all of the joyous occasions, tragic times, and every moment in between as I pored over letters, journals and photos.

I remained in our home until February of 2014, when I moved into Hearthside Place, a new assisted living complex in Eston. After a couple of years there, I moved into the Franklin Retirement Residence in Saskatoon. The Franklin was far more convenient for all of my appointments and they also had more options for care. I lived on the 9th floor and had quite a view, except for the funeral home next door; it wouldn't be too far to go when I passed on! There were a couple of short stays in and out of the hospital before I was moved into Oliver Lodge Aged Care Facility. After almost a year there, I moved for the final time into Circle Drive Alliance Care Home, in August 2019.

Some exciting news during this time was that our granddaughter, Rhea, got married (2017) and then later was expecting our first great-grand baby—due in March 2020. A baby boy, Pax, was born on March 19th, 2020, in Australia during the COVID-19 lockdown. I was so thankful on March 24th to be able to see all of my family, including the new little addition, via a video call. How wonderful to have that technology; it answered my prayer to be able to see them!

Months earlier, I had asked God why I was still on the earth. Now, I knew my time was complete. I was at peace and looking forward to finally seeing my precious Lord and Saviour. In the early hours of Friday, March 27th, 2020, I breathed my last breath on earth and was immediately in the presence of God. Oh, the glorious reunions with Phyllis, Michael and so many friends who had gone ahead earlier. My life on earth had ended; eternity just begun…

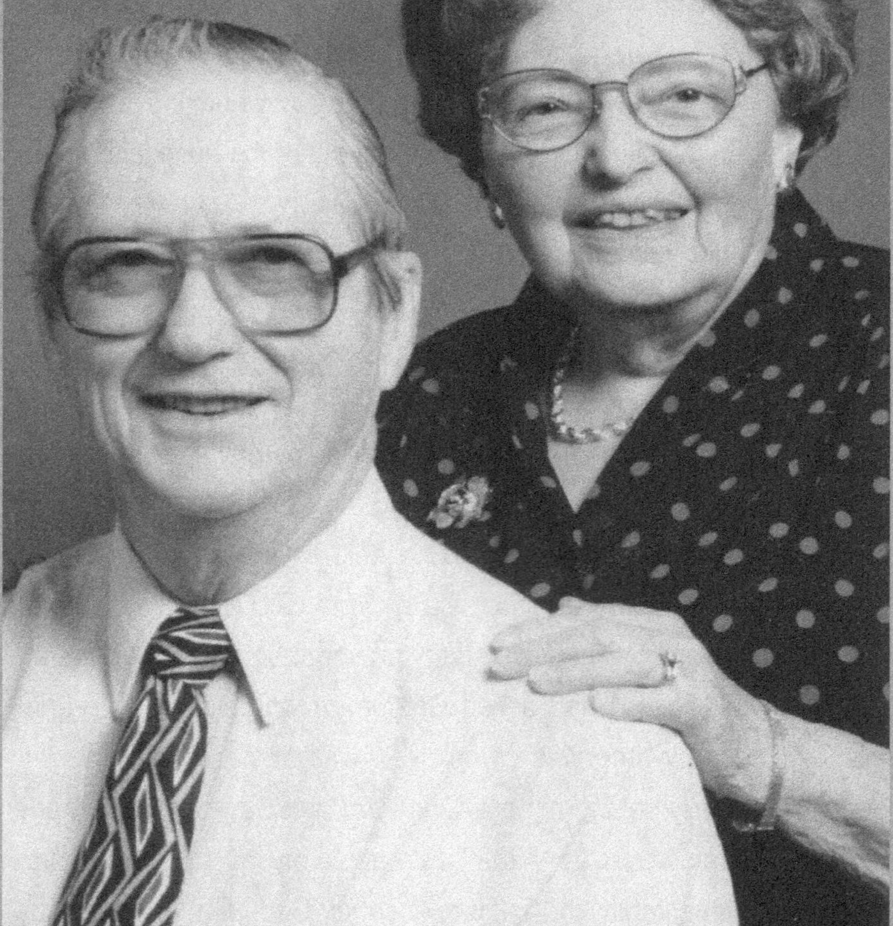

Rhonnie and Rick's Wedding, Holloway Beach, Queensland-Dec. 19, 1987

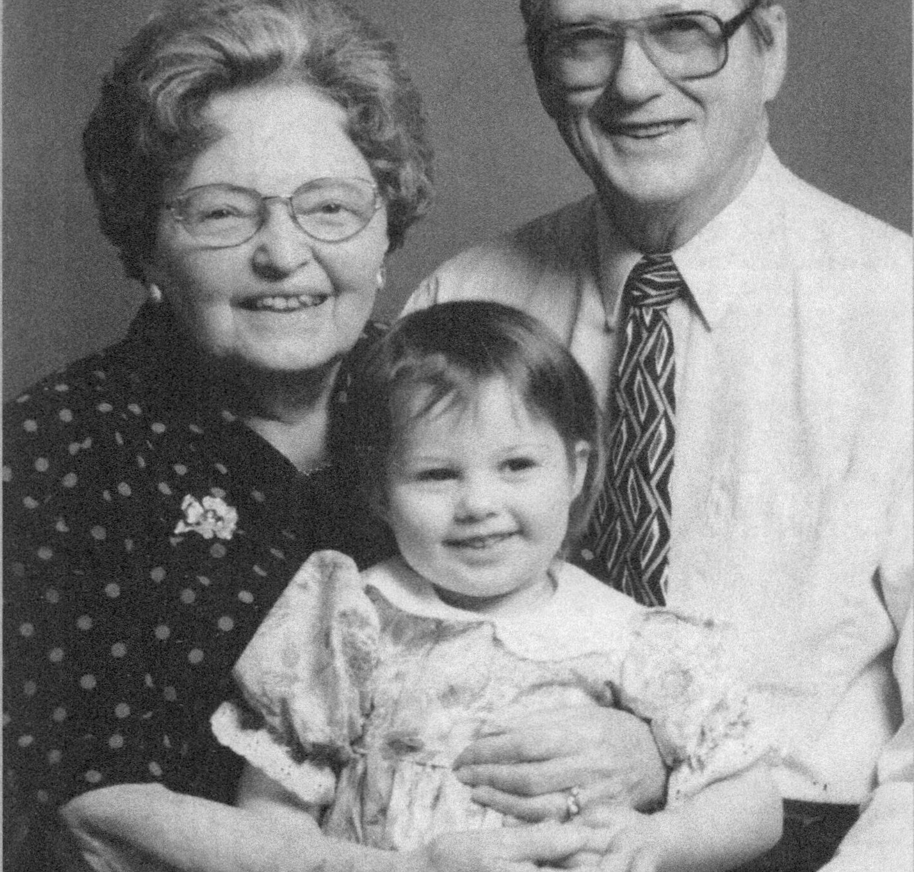

"I solemnly urge you in the presence of God and Christ Jesus, who will someday judge the living and the dead when He appears to set up His kingdom: **Preach the word of God**. Be prepared, whether the time is favorable or not. Patiently correct, rebuke, and encourage your people with good teaching. For a time is coming when people will no longer listen to sound and wholesome teaching. They will follow their own desires and will look for teachers who will tell them whatever their itching ears want to hear. They will reject the truth and chase after myths. But you should keep a clear mind in every situation. Don't be afraid of suffering for the Lord. Work at telling others the Good News, and **fully carry out the ministry God has given you**. As for me, my life has already been poured out as an offering to God. The time of my death is near. I have fought the good fight, I have finished the race, and **I have remained faithful**. And now the prize awaits me-the crown of righteousness, which the Lord, the righteous Judge, will give me on the day of His return. And the prize is not just for me but for all who eagerly look forward to His appearing."

        2 Timothy 4:1-8(NLT)

May 1979-With Mary Goforth Moynan on tour in Saskatchewan
"Didn't we have fun!"

At home, 1985 with Sam & Janet Digber and Sam & Victoria Mensah

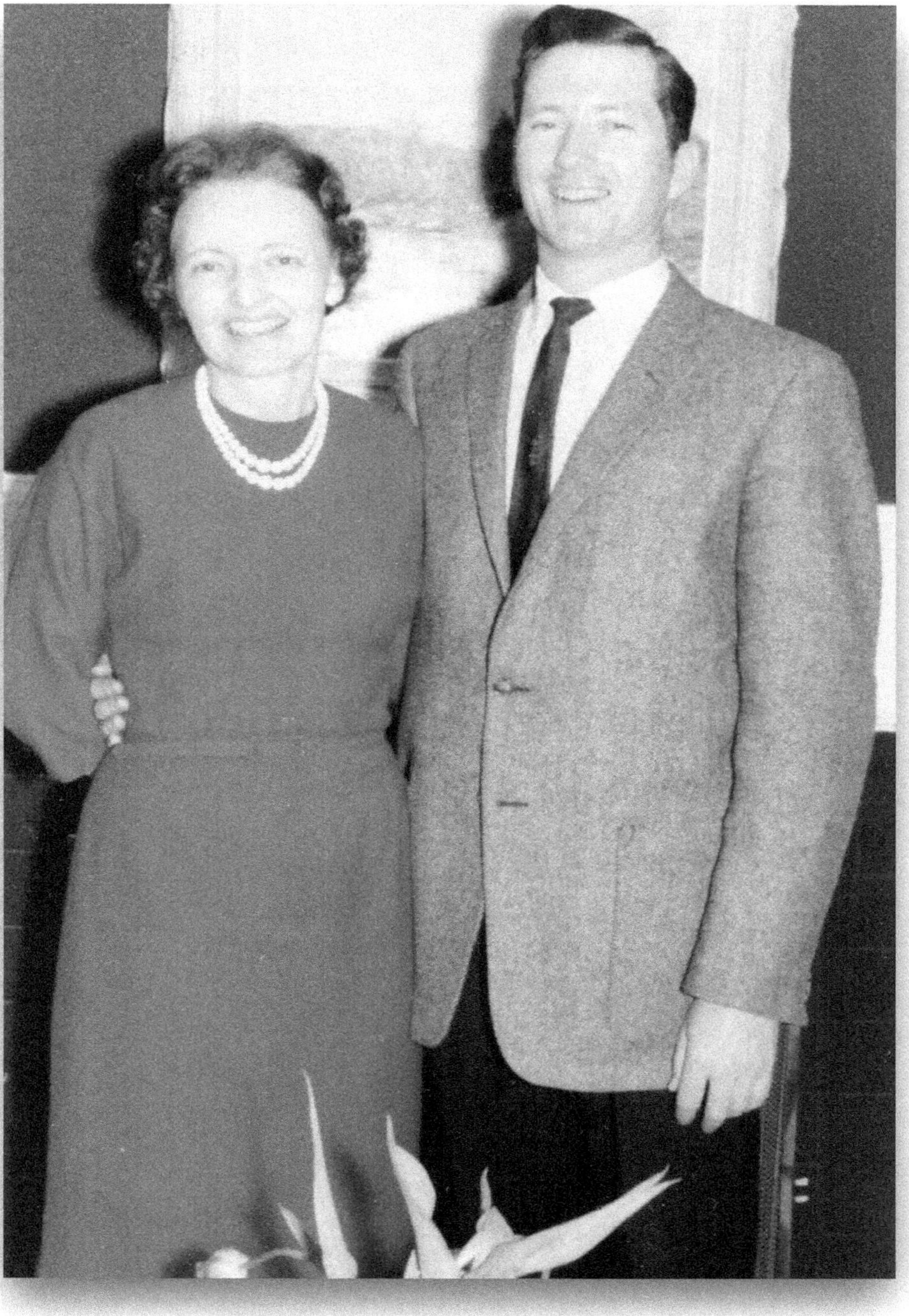

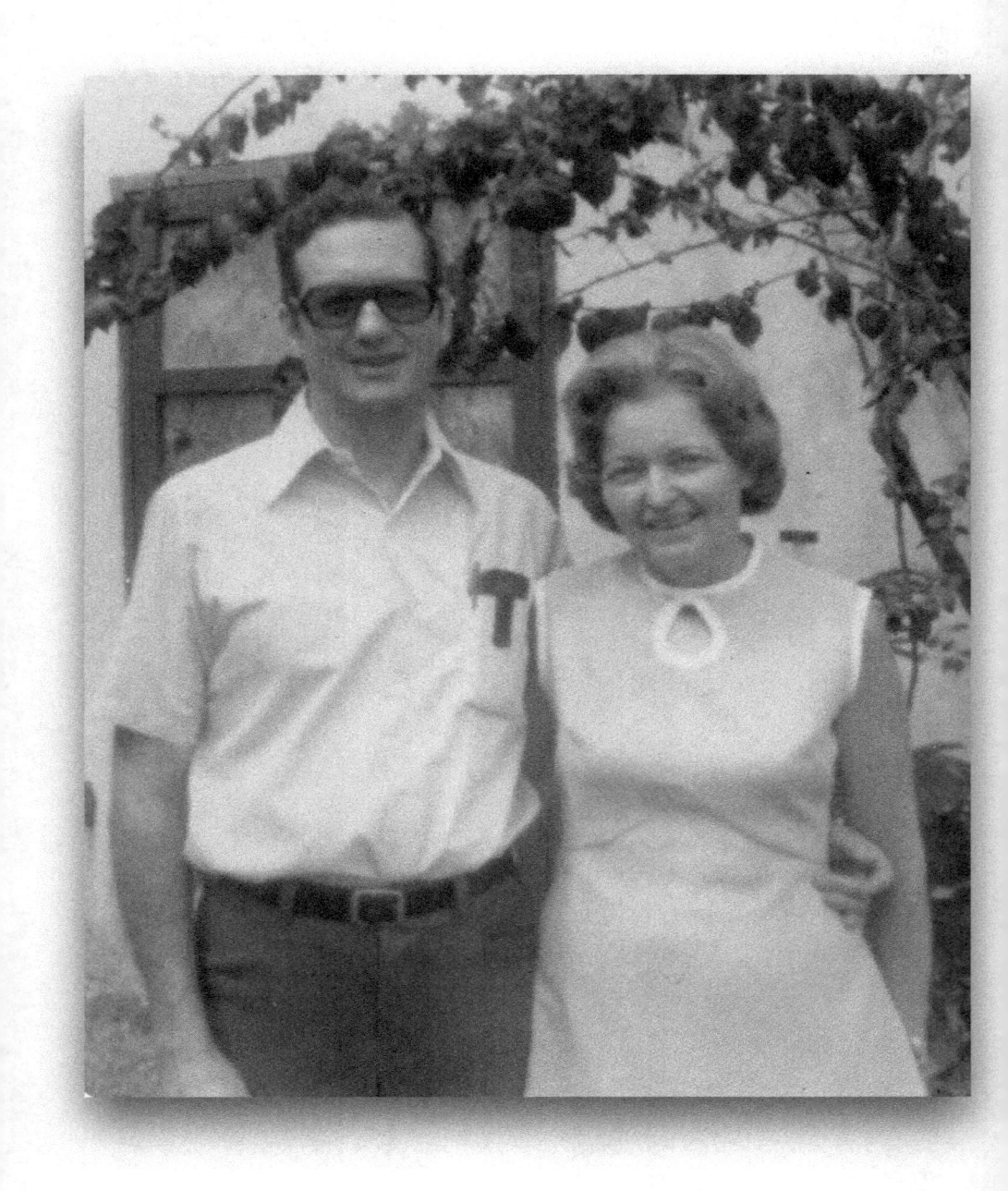

Editor's Note: Stan had written everything in this memoir, except for Chapter 41. It was the desire of the editor to write a final chapter to let the reader know the basics of what had transpired from Africa until his passing. This was accomplished from remembering past talks with Stan, checking up on Facebook, texts, reading through Grass to Grain Volumes I and II to check dates, and with immense assistance from Rhonnie. I wanted to keep the narrative in the first person for continuity. My apologies if anything is amiss. Stan worked so very hard on his memoirs and I just couldn't let them remain lost, forgotten and unpublished.

Stan had also just left these last few notes...perhaps they will jog someone's memory of the events:

Rhonnie was always a cheerful little girl, going about the house singing and dancing

Crying sitting in a highchair—snake

Playing--- with Rachel and Sarah in Boura, learning how to cook African food, hunt for condiments and other edible foods in the bush, and play games

Animals—Rhonnie reared several animals...duiker antelope, vervet monkeys, red monkeys, parrots and birds of many varieties, rabbits, guinea pigs, and cats-—monkey bite; Stan suffered a serious gash to his lower leg from one of the vervet monkeys which was "protecting" Rhonnie. He had to have a rabies shot and there was fear of infection as monkey bites can be very dangerous.

Leo—Andrew, the Senegal parrot was a much-loved member of the family and a source of great amusement. He and Rhonnie were inseparable!

Ground squirrel—"Berry" shredded Stan's Bible School notes to make a nest

Theo—the King's beloved dog

School—Rhonnie was homeschooled while in Burkina Faso. She only attended public school when on furlough in BC, and for Grade 12, when she attended an International Boarding School in Jos, Nigeria.

Rachel, Rhonnie, Sara

Woman carrying water in the pot on her head Thatched structures are granaries.

Women pounding grain-notice the cartier in the distance behind

Young girls pounding millet in a mortar, and an adult winnowing the grain to get rid of the chaff

Clockwise from far left:
Carol Lungren, Victor Hildebrandt with the King's dog Theo, Rhonnie King, Phyllis King, Clark Lungren, Raymond Hildebrandt, Helen Hildebrandt, Armien Hildebrandt, 1972

Stan, Ethel and Jim Hunter, Phyllis

Page 247

APPENDIX: RHONNIE'S STORY

Memories of my early years in Africa are very hazy. I'm not sure what I'm remembering and what I'm imagining from having heard stories or seen photographs.

My earliest "memory" is of making mud pies with Ken Hildebrandt in Kassou when I was probably 18 months to 2 years. We were living at the time in the village guest house, a round, mud, brick building with an outer wall that was only chest height affording very little privacy. When it rained, the thatched roof leaked like a sieve. We covered the mosquito netting over the bed with a plastic tablecloth to give us some protection from the rain. Snakes lived in the walls! There were no doors, only openings in the wall, so livestock wandered in and out at will.

My next memory is of the unfinished school building in Boura where we lived temporarily in the mid-1950's. I can still remember waking in the night to snuffling, grunting noises from beneath my cot which was located outside on the verandah. I screamed until my parents arrived and convinced me it was only a sow and her piglets. Another memory of life in the schoolhouse was of a rooster chasing a hen up and over the table where we were eating our meal. I also recall sitting beneath a tree while my Mother held children's services.

Next came the mud, brick house that my father built on land acquired from the village chief. It had aluminum sheeting on the roof which had yet to be nailed down and which was being held in place temporarily by large rocks. One night, while my father was away, a storm with gale-force winds ripped the sheets of tin off and the rocks fell into the rooms below. My Mother and I sheltered in a doorway to avoid being struck! The holes in the floor caused by the rocks remained as a reminder for quite some time.

We were all very fond of cats, so once we moved into the Boura house, Pipsqueak and Teddy Bear (named by myself, of course) joined the household. I watched in awe as they had a litter of kittens and the two adults and the kittens all snuggled together in a box, a picture of love and contentment. It wasn't long before we had a lot of cats!

An animal lover, I also reared baby orphaned monkeys: Vervet (green) and red patas monkey and antelope (mostly the common duiker but occasionally kob and roan). I had an aviary full of various birds including African grey parrots, finches, cordon-bleu, to name a few. My favourite was the brightly coloured, highly intelligent and amusing Senegal parrot which made a wonderful companion bird. The African grey and the Senegal parrots could mimic human language. I also had rabbits, hedgehogs and ground squirrels. We had a noisy flock of guinea fowl for eggs and meat, as well as chickens. My job after school was to scour the bush for small termite (white ant) mounds, bring them back in a bucket (pail) and break them up so the hen and chicks could eat the ants.

The bush (savannah) was my backyard. I had all my animals to feed! I would roam the bush, completely at home, with a monkey clinging to my arm or leg, my antelope trotting along behind, and my Senegal parrot on my shoulder. I knew what bush fruit and seeds were edible for humans and what was preferred by my various animals. I would return with my arms loaded with leaves and grasses, fruit and seeds for my menagerie.

I had a wonderful rapport with the local Sissala village children. The children were learning French in school so I learned French from them and also some Sissala. They taught me their games and I taught them mine (mainly tag or follow the leader). We had no toys and no TV so we used our imagination. They taught me how to make things with reeds and grasses, twigs and branches. We would race cars with long steering wheels all made from reeds. I would accompany the children into the bush when they tended the family's goat herd. While keeping a watchful eye on the herd and any strays, the children showed me which bush fruits were edible and how to build shelters from the sun.

I had two special girlfriends, Rachel and Sara, and Marc Zalve was the brother I had lost. Although Marc was from the village of Ti, he attended school in Boura and, years later, when we moved to Leo, he was in the first class of Bible School students. Tragically, Marc lost his first wife, Martine, a beautiful, happy young woman and the love of his life, giving birth to a child. The child survived and Marc eventually remarried and had more children. Even after I left Upper Volta in my late teens we continued to correspond and today we connect via Facebook and video calls.

In the afternoons after school, I loved to ride my bicycle into the village and visit my friends' homes. They lived in "cartiers" (quarters) made up of the extended family. A village consisted of several of these cartiers and each cartier was surrounded by fields. The Boura chief and his extended household (he had over 20 wives, approximately 60 children) occupied the largest cartier, and was walled.

In their homes, I watched the women prepare the evening meal and would often help them pound the millet in a wooden mortar with a pestle and stir the pot of "to" (millet porridge, pronounced 'toe'). I would often eat with them as their culture demands that every visitor be offered food and to refuse would be an insult. At mealtime, the men were served first, then the women and children ate from a communal pot, with their hands. I did likewise. I loved the hot chili peppers that were used in every sauce. And I love yams deep fried in "karite" (shea) butter. I loved the peanut chicken with rice (prepared on special occasions) and pounded yam served with okra sauce. I loved the smell of the cooking fires. I would often go with the women and children when they went to collect wood from the bush. I learned what leaves to pick for making sauce. During "karite" season, I would accompany the women and children as they gathered the fruit. The nut was dried and then turned into "butter" by a very long and arduous process that lasted days. (The karite fruit is delicious to eat. It resembles avocado in texture and when fully ripe is very sweet.) It was a wonderful time in my life!

Occasionally we would visit the other Mission Stations: Leo, Kassou, Silli, Diebougou and Batie for some "r and r". At least twice a year, all the missionaries and their children would gather at one of the stations for business meetings and Christmas. These get-togethers were a wonderful time for all, but especially for the MK's (missionary kids). We had such fun! We used our imaginations and created games of cowboys and Indians, the Swiss Family Robinson, the Jungle Book, Bambi, etc. We built forts and treehouses. The girls played at being African women carrying dolls on our backs like the African women did and cooking African food over an open fire which we'd then serve to our families. I cherish the memories of those get-togethers. We children had a special bond and nearly all of us have kept in contact. Often, when I've been in Canada, some of us have been able to catch up and when we do, we reminisce about those wonderful days of our youth.

Every four years we went on "furlough" to Canada. There I endured public school where I was very shy and terrified of being noticed by the teacher! When I wasn't in school, we travelled between New Westminster, British Columbia (my Mother's hometown) and Eston, Saskatchewan (my Father's hometown). My parents also travelled throughout Western Canada to raise funds to help support the work in Upper Volta. I hated the Canadian winters and the busyness of Canadian life. I longed to return to the simple, uncomplicated life and the friends and animals I loved in Upper Volta.

In the 50's we travelled back and forth to Africa via Europe mainly by sea on passenger liners or freighters. I have fond memories of life onboard ship. The freighters were particularly fun as there were few passengers. We ate with the Captain and Officers, consequently, the meals were superb! As the only child on board, I was showered with attention. I remember celebrating a birthday, possibly my 5th, on board and was honoured with a decorated chair at the breakfast table and gifts from many of the crew and other passengers.

Another highlight was the time we spent living in a

"Pension" (shared lodging with board) in Lausanne, Switzerland. All three of us were enrolled in French language school. Most of the other residents at the Pension were also language students. The meals were out of this world, even by my 9-year-old standards! I had my own room with a balcony overlooking a beautiful park. We spent our weekends exploring Lac Leman (or Lake Geneva as it is also known), and the surrounding countryside. It was very mountainous and incredibly beautiful. We visited the famous Chateau de Chillon, picturesque Montreux, the Nestle factory at Vevey, Rocher de Naye and the beautiful lakeside promenade in Lausanne. I think I must have developed my love of French-style cuisine while living in Lausanne. We provided our own lunches which consisted of a variety of wonderful cheeses, pate, baguette or brioche, olives, pastries, Petit Gervais or Petit Suisse, Yoplait yogurt and luscious fruits such as strawberries. It was an amazing time in my life! When we lived in Upper Volta, as it was known then, because it was a French colony in the 1950s and '60s, French cuisine was available to us when we were in Ouagadougou, the capital. It was such a treat for us to visit a French Patisserie or dine at a French Restaurant (our favourite restaurant in Ouaga was Eau Vive run by nuns).

    I was homeschooled, following a Canadian curriculum by correspondence. My parents felt this was best so that when we returned to Canada on furlough I would fit in better with Canadian schools. My mother was a schoolteacher so I was in good hands in the early years. However, after our move to Leo, both of my parents became heavily involved with the Bible School, language classes and the young women's shelter while still maintaining regular contact with the Sissala churches they had pioneered. Consequently, I was left to my own devices and I'm afraid that there were just too many distractions! By Grade 11 I was struggling, particularly with math, and was falling behind generally. So, in 1971, I was sent to Jos, Nigeria, to attend Hillcrest International Christian Boarding School. It was an eventful year at Hillcrest. I boarded at the Assemblies of God house and gradually I overcame my shyness. I even taught French to a Primary School class. I graduated in 1972 and returned to Upper Volta. Soon after, much against my will, I left my beloved Africa to attend FGBI in Eston, Canada the Bible College in my Dad's hometown where he and my mother had met and begun their journey.

I attended FGBI for one year then moved to Vancouver and enrolled in the University of British Columbia to study Linguistics, graduating with honours in 1978. The summer between FGBI and UBC I lived in Banff, Alberta and worked in a gift shop. That summer was a wonderful experience, far removed from my life in the bush of Africa. Banff remains one of my favourite places in Canada. Rarely do I visit Canada without stopping in Banff!

After a couple of years working at the Canadian Imperial Bank of Commerce (CIBC) in Vancouver, I successfully applied for a position with Revenue Canada Taxation. I loved the job and I made lasting friends at Revenue Canada, but I felt as though I was stagnating and felt very unfulfilled and unhappy living in Canada. This was not my home and I longed to return to Africa. I did return, but only for a visit, and had a wonderful reunion with my friends there.

From my early childhood in Upper Volta, I corresponded with a penpal in Fiji named Rajendra Prakash. With two weeks' annual holidays available, I wrote to Rajen and said that I would like to meet him and his family after fifteen years of corresponding. He replied from Brisbane, Queensland, Australia to inform me that he was now married and that he and Sharon had moved to Australia and that I was welcome to visit. I was disappointed as Australia wasn't on the list of countries I wanted to visit. It was arranged that I would spend a week with him and Sharon in Brisbane and a week in Fiji where I would meet his family. In early 1982 I arrived in Brisbane, never imagining that Australia was to become my future home!

Upon my return to Canada, I immediately applied for a Working Holiday Visa for Australia and a leave of absence from my job at Revenue Canada. The Lord had a hand upon my life because I was granted both. By the end of 1982, I was travelling back to Australia and my life took a whole new, exciting direction. I am now an Australian/Canadian dual citizen and married to Rick Wenden, a New Zealander I met on an island near the Great Barrier Reef off the coast of Queensland. We have a beautiful daughter, Rhea, and an adorable grandson, Pax. I have enjoyed the most exciting, happy life since making Australia my permanent home. I have lived and worked on beautiful, tropical Keppel Island, where Rick and I met; Rick and I have owned a restaurant in Cairns and I have managed numerous tour and travel agencies. As a tour and travel agent, I have travelled around Australia and overseas, I have experienced the Great Barrier Reef and Islands, I have participated in extreme sports and have experienced first hand everything there is to see and do in Tropical North Queensland. Cairns has been our home for 34 years (2021) and I wouldn't live anywhere else. Here I have the best of both worlds-a tropical climate in modern, first-world culture. I visited Burkina Faso once again, from Australia, in 1987, and it was wonderful to renew old acquaintances in the Sissala villages of my childhood, as well as in Leo, Ouagadougou and Koudougou, although, sadly, some of my friends had passed on. A piece of my heart will always be there, and, thanks to Social Media, I am able to keep in contact, mainly with the younger generation, the children of my childhood friends.

When I first moved to Australia, my parents were still living in Africa. They had started their ministry in Ghana and were commuting between Leo and Accra. My mother returned to Canada for health reasons and purchased a house in Eston. Dad remained in Africa but for shorter periods. By 1990 his health had deteriorated. Years of being exposed to dust took a toll on his lungs and the effects of meningitis that had nearly claimed his life in Sierra Leone all those years ago were causing health issues. He returned to Eston permanently.

My only regret, living in Australia, was the distance from our aging parents, mine and Rick's. For years we travelled to both New Zealand and Canada to spend time with both sets of parents. In August 1997 Rick was offered a job on a ranch in Alberta owned by friends of ours. Rhea and I joined him in January 1998 and stayed until November 1999. During this time, we were able to see a lot of my parents. Later, my mother, Phyllis, visited us in New Zealand

and Cairns on two occasions, and twice my Mom and Dad made the long, tiring journey to Australia together, in 1996, when Rhea was 6 months and again in 2001, when Rhea was five. After that, we continued to visit them in Canada regularly.

Rick lost both of his parents and in 2012 I lost my Mother. Rhea and I attended her funeral in Eston in the middle of a brutally cold winter! Even Vancouver was having a record cold spell with snow on the ground for over 20 consecutive days. We were very glad to return to our tropical paradise in Cairns!

With my mother gone, I asked Dad if he would consider moving to Australia. After careful consideration, he declined so I promised Dad that I would visit him every year and I did, until 2020 when COVID-19 prevented me.

The house in Eston was sold and Dad moved to a tiny unit in a four plex as he waited for Hearthside, an Assisted Living Home in Eston, to be completed. He was in Hearthside for a short time before it became apparent that he needed to be closer to medical facilities in Saskatoon, a two-hour drive away. During my annual visit, in answer to prayer, we found the Franklin Retirement Home in downtown Saskatoon. It ticked all the boxes, including the "pet-friendly" box so that he was able to keep his faithful companion, Shadow.

Dad was diagnosed with congestive heart failure and was in and out of the hospital so it soon became apparent that he required more assistance. Rhea visited him at this time and was instrumental in getting him assessed and approved for an Aged Care Facility. With no idea when there was likely to be a vacancy in a Home, I booked a ticket from Australia, arriving in Saskatoon on a Friday, and Dad was accepted into Oliver Lodge on the Monday. Once again, God answered prayer! I moved into his suite at the Franklin as the rent was paid up to the end of the month, and began the task of downsizing, as he could only keep the barest of essential items. He insisted that he needed his laptop and printer, as he was writing his memoirs, so he was moved to a larger room at Oliver Lodge to accommodate his request.

  The following year was the last move—to a Christian Alliance Aged Care Facility that he had requested while still at the Franklin. By this time, he was struggling to breathe and had become very weak, as the congestive heart failure worsened. When I left him in September 2019, I didn't know if I would see him alive again and I didn't. COVID-19 stopped me from getting to his bedside in March 2020. We did the next best thing. With the help of staff at Christian Alliance, all four of us, Rhea, her husband, Drew, Rick and I spoke with him and introduced him to his newborn great-grandson, Pax. Dad passed away two days later, with his nephew Rod Pritchard, and Rod's wife, Gwen, by his side; singing and praying and reading scripture as he passed on.

I know that the Lord welcomed him with open arms, proclaiming "well done, good and faithful servant." (Matthew 25:21 NIV)

Rhonnie, Leo, 1966

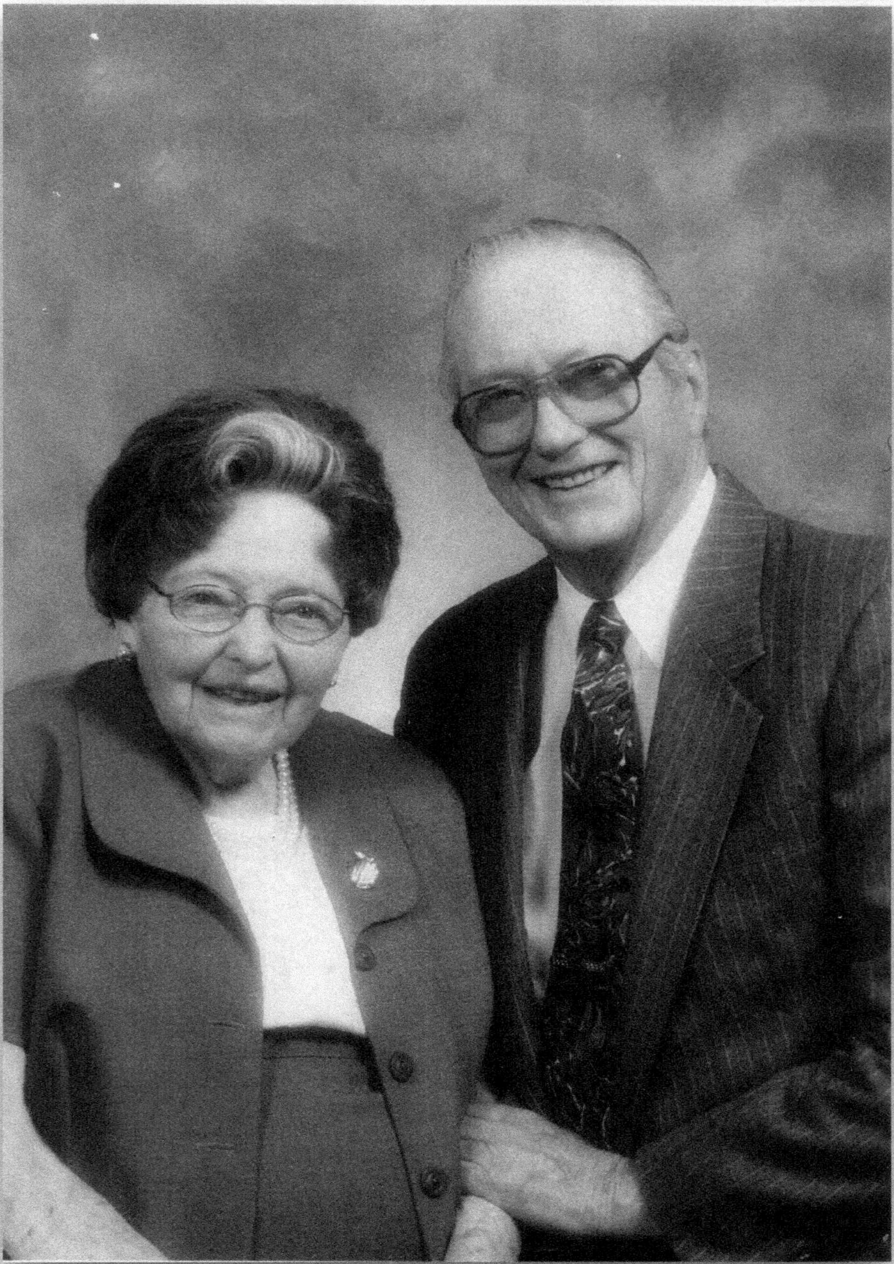